Introducing Mechanisms and APIs for Memory Management

Using Windows OS Native Runtime APIs

Roger Villela

Apress®

Introducing Mechanisms and APIs for Memory Management: Using Windows OS Native Runtime APIs

Roger Villela
Sao Paulo, São Paulo, Brazil

ISBN-13 (pbk): 978-1-4842-5415-8
https://doi.org/10.1007/978-1-4842-5416-5

ISBN-13 (electronic): 978-1-4842-5416-5

Managing Director, Apress Media LLC: Welmoed Spahr
Acquisitions Editor: Smriti Srivastava
Development Editor: Matthew Moodie
Coordinating Editor: Shrikant Vishwakarma

Cover designed by eStudioCalamar

Cover image designed by Freepik (www.freepik.com)

Distributed to the book trade worldwide by Springer Science+Business Media New York, 233 Spring Street, 6th Floor, New York, NY 10013. Phone 1-800-SPRINGER, fax (201) 348-4505, e-mail orders-ny@springer-sbm.com, or visit www.springeronline.com. Apress Media, LLC is a California LLC and the sole member (owner) is Springer Science + Business Media Finance Inc (SSBM Finance Inc). SSBM Finance Inc is a **Delaware** corporation.

For information on translations, please e-mail rights@apress.com, or visit www.apress.com/rights-permissions.

Apress titles may be purchased in bulk for academic, corporate, or promotional use. eBook versions and licenses are also available for most titles. For more information, reference our Print and eBook Bulk Sales web page at www.apress.com/bulk-sales.

Any source code or other supplementary material referenced by the author in this book is available to readers on GitHub via the book's product page, located at www.apress.com/978-1-4842-5415-8. For more detailed information, please visit www.apress.com/source-code.

Printed on acid-free paper

This book is dedicated to my mother,
Marina Roel de Oliveira.[†]

[†]*From 1952, January 14 to 2017, March 17*

Table of Contents

About the Author

 **Roger Villela** is a software engineer and entrepreneur with almost 30 years of experience in the industry. Currently, he specializes in the inner works of the orthogonal features of the following Microsoft development platforms:

- Microsoft Windows operating system base services

- Microsoft Universal Windows Platform (UWP)

- Microsoft WinRT

- Microsoft .NET Framework implementation of the runtime environment (CLR)

His work is based on Microsoft Visual Studio (Microsoft Windows) and Intel Parallel Studio XE (Microsoft Windows), using the following programming languages, extensions, and projections:

- C/C++

- Assembly (Intel IA-32/Intel 64 [x64/amd64])

- Component Extensions for runtimes (C++/CLI and C++/CX)

About the Technical Reviewer

 **Carsten Thomsen** is primarily a back-end developer but works with smaller front-end bits as well. He has authored and reviewed a number of books and has created numerous Microsoft Learning courses, all related to software development. He works as a freelancer/contractor in various countries in Europe, using Azure, Visual Studio, Azure DevOps, and GitHub. An exceptional troubleshooter, he asks the right questions, in a most logical to least logical fashion. Carsten also enjoys working with architecture, research, analysis, development, testing, and bug fixing. Carsten is an excellent communicator with great mentoring and team-lead skills.

Acknowledgments

First I would like to thank the team from Apress who worked with me on this book: Smriti Srivastava (Acquisitions Editor), Shrikant Vishwakarma (Coordinating Editor), Matthew Moodie (Development Editor), Welmoed Spahr (Managing Director), and Carsten Thomsen (Technical Reviewer). It was a pleasure and an honor to work with such a highly professional, committed, and motivated team.

Thanks to all my parents and a special thanks to my brother Eder, my brother Marlos and his wife Janaína, my nephew Gabriel, and my nieces Lívia and Rafaela.

I would like to thank my professional colleagues and friends who have worked with me over the years.

Introduction

The book is about memory management mechanisms and APIs. It begins with introductory topics about the hardware features on the Intel x86 and Intel 64 (x64/amd64) hardware architectures related to memory management. You will be working with C++ programming language features such as pointers, C++ Standard Library smart pointers, and Microsoft UCRT functionalities for memory management.

Specifically, the book discusses how to use pointers when using the C++ programming language and how to use smart pointers through the C++ programming language, as well as the unique_ptr, shared_ptr, and weak_ptr C++ Standard Library template-based types.

A fundamental library for memory management on the Microsoft Windows native platform is available through the Microsoft UCRT and Microsoft CRT implementations. The book also covers functions for manipulating memory management via Microsoft UCRT/CRT.

Regardless of whether or not you have basic knowledge of memory management via Microsoft Windows native programming and the C++ programming language, if you need to learn about memory management, this book is for you.

CHAPTER 1

Memory Management

This chapter introduces memory management from the perspective of the technologies available through the Intel IA-32 (32-bit) architecture and the Intel 64 (x64/amd64) architecture.

Acronyms

The following acronyms are used in this chapter:

- Advanced Programmable Interrupt Controller (APIC)

- Intel Architecture (IA)

- Physical Address Extensions (PAE)

- System Management Interrupt (SMI)

- System Management Mode (SMM)

Understanding Hardware

To be able to program code in a memory management context, you require knowledge of the hardware architecture at some level.

To help with these first steps, this chapter presents introductory information about the concepts and functionalities of two real computer processor architectures: Intel IA-32 (32-bit) and Intel 64 (x64/amd64, 64-bit).

© Roger Villela 2020
R. Villela, *Introducing Mechanisms and APIs for Memory Management*,
https://doi.org/10.1007/978-1-4842-5416-5_1

The IA-32 (32-bit) and Intel 64 (64-bit) processor architectures have specific hardware and programming facilities for memory management. This means that the operating system and programs should use these hardware and programming facilities to access the memory with efficiency and reliability.

These facilities are available via a combination of the following: a processor architecture, a processor mode of operation, and a processor memory model.

Processor Architecture

This section introduces the memory management facilities based on two processor architectures.

- IA-32 for 32-bit processor implementation

- Intel 64 (x64/amd64) for 64-bit processor implementation

The following are the basic characteristics of the IA-32 Intel386 processor implementation:

- It is a 32-bit processor implementation.

- The 32-bit address bus of the processor can map and work with up to 4 GB of physical memory.

- It can work with a range of physical memory addresses from 0 to $2^{32}-1$.

- It can support paging as a mechanism for the implementation of virtual memory management.

- It can work with a range of physical memory addresses from 0 to 2^36-1 using special extensions of the Intel processor, called PAE, that are part of the features of the paging mechanism.

- The processor provides a virtual-8086 mode that allows the execution of programs written for the 8086 and 8088 processors, which are both 16-bit.

- The lower half of each 32-bit Intel386 register retains properties of the 16-bit registers of earlier generations of processors, permitting backward compatibility.

The following are the basic characteristics of the Intel 64 (x64/amd64) Intel Core processor family implementation:

- It is a 64-bit processor implementation.

- The 64-bit address bus of the processor can map and work with more than 4 GB of physical memory.

- It can work with a range of physical memory addresses from 0 to 2^64-1.

- It can support paging as a mechanism for the implementation of virtual memory management.

- The processor is compatible with running software written for 16-bit and 32-bit.

Processor Mode of Operation

An IA-32 processor or Intel 64 (x64/amd64) processor has a *mode of operation*, which determines which architectural features and assembly instructions will be available.

The IA-32 processor architecture implementation supports three modes of operation.

- *Protected mode* is the native mode of operation of the processor.

- *Real-address mode* is the mode of operation that implements the Intel 8086 processor programming environment. A processor that implements the IA-32 architecture is configured automatically to real-address mode following power-up or a reset. From real-address mode, it is also possible to switch to protected mode or to SMM, and this switching capability is part of a set of extensions and is not available in the original Intel 8086 programming environment.

- System management mode provides to the operating system or executive environment a transparent mechanism for implementing functions that are platform-specific such as power management and security for the system. The processor enters SMM when the external SMM interrupt pin, named SMI in the hardware scheme, is activated or an SMM interrupt is received from the APIC device. The SMM was introduced with the Intel 386 SL and Intel 486 SL processors and became the standard for the IA-32 architecture of the Intel Pentium family of processors.

The Intel 64 (x64) architecture adds the IA-32e mode of operation. The IA-32e mode of operation has two submodes of operation.

- The compatibility mode of operation (a submode of the IA-32e mode) enables most 16-bit and 32-bit applications and libraries to run without recompilation under a 64-bit operating system implementation.

When talking about an IA-32 architecture (32-bit), the compatibility 64-bit submode of operation is referred to only as *compatibility mode*. This submode is similar in terms of functionality to the IA-32 architecture's protected mode, because it uses only the first 4 GB of memory linear address space and uses 16-bit and 32-bit operand sizes.

- The 64-bit mode of operation (a submode of IA-32e mode) enables a 64-bit operating system implementation to run applications written to access the full 64-bit linear address space. When talking about an IA-32 architecture (32-bit), the 64-bit submode of operation is referred to only as *64-bit mode*.

Processor Memory Models

This section introduces the processor memory models.

Memory Models and the IA-32 Architecture

When using the memory management facilities of an IA-32 (32-bit) architecture, the executing code does not directly access the physical memory. This access to physical memory is made through a *memory model*.

The IA-32 (32-bit) architecture provides three memory models when running on the protected mode of operation, which is the native mode of operation of the processor.

- Flat

- Segmented

- Real-address

5

Flat Memory Model

In this memory model, the physical memory appears to the executing code as a single and continuous address space that is called the *linear address space*.

This linear address space ranges from 0 to 2^32-1 (4GB) and is byte addressable.

An address for a byte in this linear address space is called the *linear address*.

In this memory model, every kind of information is contained in this same linear address space, without a scheme for isolation or protection.

This means that the code, data, and stacks are not isolated from each other by some hardware protection mechanism, and one section of code can inadvertently write into the area of another section of code, data, or stack, creating serious protection violations and breaking the operating system and program functionalities.

Figure 1-1 can help you visualize these concepts of the flat model, namely, the linear address space and the linear address.

Figure 1-1. *Flat memory model*

Segmented Memory Model

In this memory model, the physical memory appears to the executing code as independent address spaces, with each one abstractly called a *segment address space*.

Programs running on the IA-32 processor support up to 16,383 segment address spaces of different sizes and purposes.

Each segment address space can range from 0 to $2^{32}-1$ (4GB) and is byte addressable.

In this memory model, every kind of contextual information is contained in a purpose-oriented and specific segment address space, with a scheme for isolation and protection.

This means that we have a code segment, data segment, and stack segment, as shown in Figure 1-2, isolated from each other by hardware isolation and a protection mechanism.

Code Segment
Data Segment
Stack Segment
Data Segment
Data Segment
Data Segment

Figure 1-2. *Examples of kinds of segments*

An address for a byte in this segmented address spaces is called a *logical address*, and it consists of a segment selector and an offset. (The logical address is also called a *far pointer* in various technical texts about programming APIs for the Microsoft Windows operating system.)

To access a logical address, it is necessary for a translation operation to be made transparently and automatically by the processor, which provides a segment selector and an offset.

- The segment selector indicates which kind of segment it is, such as code, data, or stack, for example.

- The offset indicates the starting byte in the address space that should be accessed through the segment selector where the information is stored.

The defined segments internally are mapped into the processor's linear address space. To access a memory location, the processor automatically translates each logical address into a linear address.

The main purpose of the segmented memory model is to provide reliability, avoiding scenarios such as the stack segment growing into the code or data address space and overwriting the instructions or data, for example.

Figure 1-3 can help you visualize these concepts of the segmented model: logical address, linear address space, and linear address.

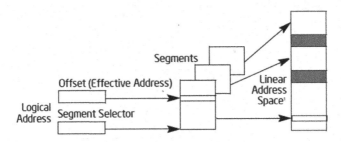

Figure 1-3. Segmented memory model

Real-Address Memory Model

In this memory model, the physical memory appears to the executing code like in the Intel 8086 processor environment.

Programs written to run on an Intel 8086 processor and running on the IA-32 processor use this memory model for compatibility. This is an emulation of the Intel 8086 processor environment.

The maximum range for the linear address space in this memory model is from 0 to 2^20-1 (1GB) and is byte addressable.

Internally, this memory model is implemented using a specialized implementation of the segmented memory model in which the linear address space is organized as an array of segments, with 64 KB as the maximum size for each one.

In this memory model, every kind of information is contained in a purpose-oriented and specific segment address space, with a scheme for isolation and protection.

This means that we have a code segment, data segment, and stack segment isolated from each other by a hardware protection mechanism.

An address for a byte in this segmented address space is called a *logical address.*

Figure 1-4 can help you visualize these concepts of the real-address mode model: logical address, linear address space, and linear address.

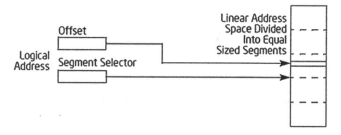

Figure 1-4. *Real-address mode memory model*

Memory Models and the Intel 64 Architecture

When using the memory management facilities of the Intel 64 (64-bit) architecture, the executing code does not directly access the physical memory. This access to physical memory is made through a *memory model.*

When on an Intel 64 processor, we can use one of these two modes of operation:

- Compatibility mode

- 64-bit mode

When on a 64-bit mode of operation, the segmentation is disabled almost completely, and the executing code sees the 64-bit flat linear address space.

Figure 1-5 can help you visualize these concepts of the flat model for 64-bit: linear address space and linear address.

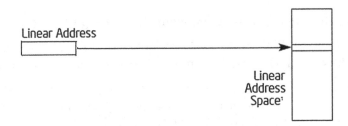

Figure 1-5. *Flat memory model for 64-bit mode*

Paging, Physical and Linear Address Spaces

For the processor, the recognized physical memory is the memory that the processor can address, map, and work with through its physical bus lines, called the *address bus*.

All physical memory mapped to the processor through its address bus lines forms what is called the *address space*.

This range of unique physical addresses is called the *physical space*.

This address space is flat (unsegmented), and for both the IA-32 and Intel 64 (x64) architectures, the physical memory is organized as a sequence of 8-bit bytes.

Each 8-bit byte has assigned a unique address called the *physical address*.

This mapping of the physical memory can be made directly or via paging.

- **Directly**: When paging is disabled, this mapping is made directly, and a one-to-one table of address correspondence is automatically created by a processor mechanism. Each linear address is sent out to the processor's bus address lines without any specialized translations.

- **Paging**: This is a mechanism for mapping and translating memory address contexts. When paging is enabled, this mapping is made through a fundamental concept and data structure called a *page*. The set of all memory addresses mapped through this paging mechanism is called the *linear address space*, and each individual memory address is called a *linear address*. Each page has a defined size (typically 4 KB but can be 4 MB or even bigger as 1 TB), and the total number of pages depend of the range of linear addresses being mapped. A page forms the virtual tables for creating the mapping between the linear addresses and the processor's physical bus lines. Collectively, all these pages form what is called *virtual memory*, where each linear address is sent out to the processor's bus address lines using a translation that is part of the paging mechanism and transparent to the programs. The paging mechanism provides the implementation of a *virtual memory system* where sections of programs are mapped into physical memory on demand, thus providing a larger linear address space to be simulated with a small amount of memory and the use of some disk storage.

For the IA-32 (32-bit) architecture, the physical addresses can range from 0 to $2^{32}-1$ (4 GB) and from 0 to $2^{36}-1$ (64 GB) when using the PAE paging mechanism.

The PAE is used by the IA-32 architecture to access more memory than 4 GB, up to 64 GB in linear address space.

The PAE technology is part of the set of paging facilities and was introduced with the Intel Pentium Pro processor.

For the Intel 64 (64-bit) architecture, the physical addresses can range from 0 to 2^64-1, and the PAE paging mechanism is active all the time for the mapping between the linear address space and the physical address space.

The PAE is used by the Intel 64 architecture to map and access the linear address space in the 0 to 2^64-1 range. However, a processor implementing the Intel 64 architecture can implement less than 64 bits for the supported range of the physical addresses.

CHAPTER 2

Development Environments, Memory Management, and Composite Type Pointers

In this chapter, I'll introduce some concepts that will be explored throughout this book. Specifically, I'll introduce the development environments used throughout this book, memory management, and the abstract concept of composite type pointers in various programming languages.

I will be using the following programming languages in this book:

- C++ as the primary programming language

- Assembly programming language

© Roger Villela 2020
R. Villela, *Introducing Mechanisms and APIs for Memory Management*,
https://doi.org/10.1007/978-1-4842-5416-5_2

Acronyms

These are the acronyms introduced in this chapter:

- International Standard Organization (ISO)

- Microsoft Visual C++ Compiler (MSVC)

Development Environments

Let's look at the development environments that are used for the
sample projects in this book. In Figure 2-1, you can see the development
environment and tools on my computer.

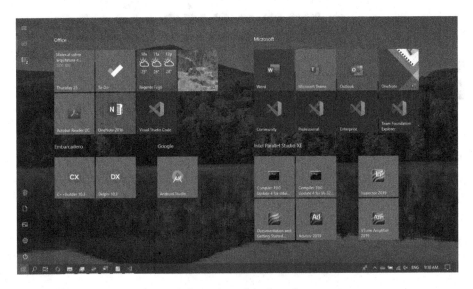

Figure 2-1. *My computer showing the development
environment tools*

These are the fundamental technologies and products:

- Microsoft Windows 10 Professional (64-bit) 1903.

- Microsoft Visual Studio 2019 16.3.1 (released to download in September 2019), any of the following editions: Community, Professional or Enterprise.

- Microsoft Visual C++. Throughout the book you'll see examples of projects configured and compiled with different tool sets from the Microsoft Visual Studio development environment.

- Intel C++ 19 (Intel Parallel Studio 2019 XE Cluster edition Update 5) integrated with the Microsoft Visual Studio 2019 16.3.1 IDE.

- Microsoft Visual C++ 2019 with Platform Toolset configured for Visual Studio 2019 (v142).

- Microsoft Visual C++ 2019 with Platform Toolset conf configured for Visual Studio 2017 (v141).

- Microsoft Visual C++ 2019 with Platform Toolset configured for Visual Studio 2017 – Windows XP (v141_xp).

- Microsoft Visual C++ 2019 with Platform Toolset configured for Visual Studio 2015 (v140).

- Microsoft Visual C++ 2019 with Platform Toolset configured for Visual Studio 2015 – Windows XP (v140_xp).

- Microsoft Visual C++ 2019 with Platform Toolset configured for LLVM (clang-cl).

Figure 2-2 shows these options.

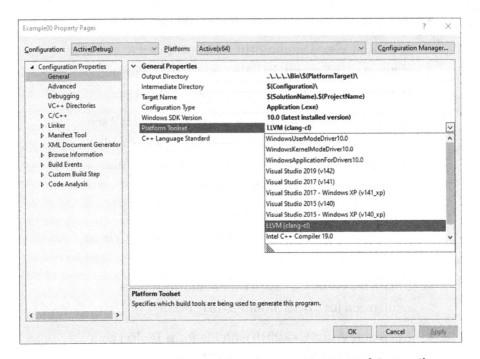

Figure 2-2.   *List of compilers and tool sets with LLVM (clang-cl)*
highlighted

Figure 2-3 shows the Windows SDK options.

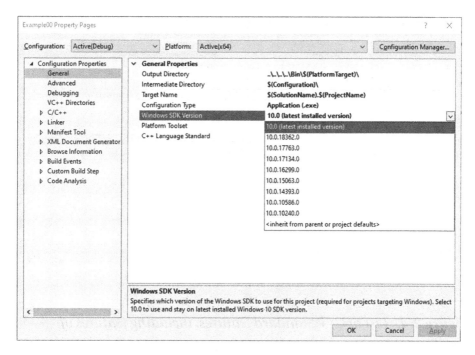

Figure 2-3. *List of Windows SDK and tool sets*

Finally, Figure 2-4 shows the ISO C++ Standard version. Despite these
options, not every combination is possible. For example, when using
Microsoft Visual Studio 2015, the Windows SDK version for Microsoft
Windows 7 is assumed and automatically changed to this number.

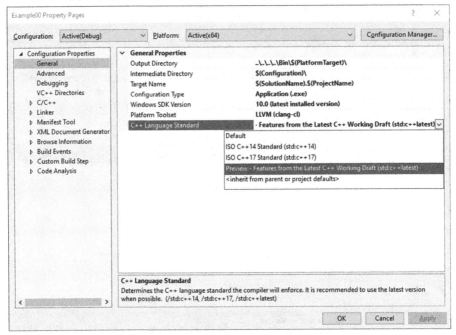

Figure 2-4. *List of C++ Standard features, including features of C++20*

The only requirement for sample projects is to have the C++ as the primary programming language for Microsoft Visual C++ 2019, the MSVC tool set v142, and C++17 set to the default configuration.

About Composite Type Pointers

In Chapter 1, I introduced composite type pointers (CTPs) and other concepts. In this chapter, you'll learn more details about CTPs and how they behave when using with different C++ tool sets.

Listing 2-1 shows a C++ code snippet with just four defined variables, initialized with the default value, in this case, nullptr. The empty braces, {}, are used in this case.

Listing 2-1. C++ Code with Only Four Variables Defined

```
#include <cstdlib>
#include <cstdint>

using namespace std;

void wmain() {

        uint32_t* ptrToUINT32{};

        int32_t* ptrToINT32{};

        uint64_t* ptrToUINT64{};

        int64_t* ptrToINT64{};

            return;
};
```

Open the solution shown in Figure 2-5 from <install_folder>\ \ IntroducingMechanismsAndAPIsForMemoryManagement\Ch02\Platforms\ Windows\Code\WE - CPP\Pointers\Example00 x86\Pointers.sln and use the project called Example00.vcxproj.

19

In the Solution Explorer window, you can see solution folders named
Example00 x64 and Example00 x86, both containing a single project that is
named after the solution folder, Example00.

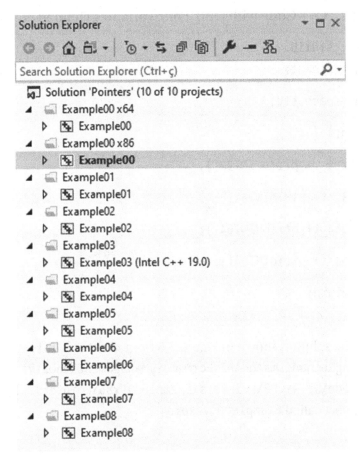

Figure 2-5. *Solution Explorer window with folder Example00 x86
containing project Example00 configured for x86 target architecture*

Figure 2-6 shows the Property Pages dialog box for the project with the standard configuration defined that we will use in the sample project in this book.

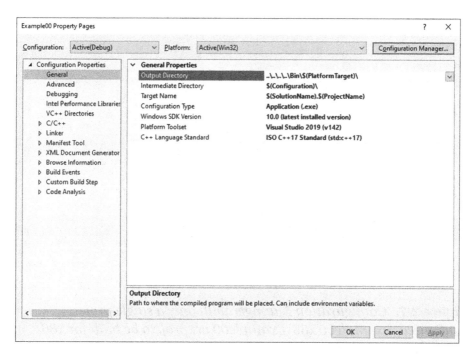

Figure 2-6. *Property Pages dialog box for the project Example00 x86\Example00.vcxproj with the Windows SDK set to 10.0.18362.1 (latest installed version), MSVC set to Visual Studio 2019 (v142), and language set to ISO C++17 Standard*

Open the Configuration Manager dialog box, and check that only one
project is configured to be built for x86 (IA-32), as shown in Figure 2-7.

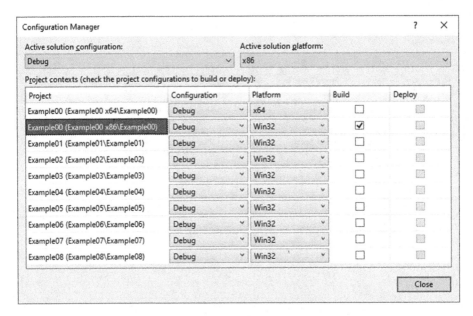

Figure 2-7. *Configuration Manager with only a single project
configured, Example00 x86\Example00.vcxproj, to be built for x86
(IA-32) as the target platform*

With the basic configuration completed, it is time to build the project.
Figure 2-8 shows the result of compilation.

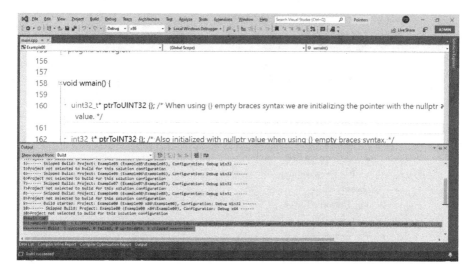

Figure 2-8. *Result of compilation of Example00 x86\Example00.
vcxproj*

To see the effect when using different C++ tool sets, change the C++
compiler toolset to LLVM (clang-cl), as shown in Figure 2-9, but keep the
other settings as is. When building the same sample project, Example00
x86\Example00, using the C++ tool set called LLVM (clang-cl), you will see
different results, as shown in Figure 2-10 and Figure 2-11.

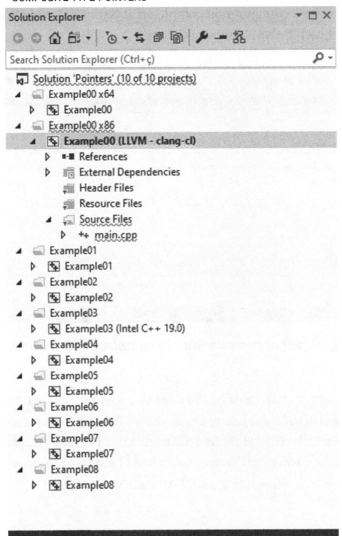

Figure 2-9. *Solution Explorer window with green squiggly lines,
indicating warnings shown for the Example00 x86\Example00.
vcxproj sample project*

```
Output                                                                                                    ▾ ▯ ✕
Show output from: Build              ▾ | 🎦 | ⇌ | ⏱ ⏱ | 필 | 🗗
9>main.cpp(164,12): warning :       unused variable 'ptrToINT32' [-Wunused-variable]
9>main.cpp(162,11): warning :            int32_t* ptrToINT32 {}; /* Also initialized with nullptr value when using {} empty braces syntax. */
9>main.cpp(162,11): warning :       unused variable 'ptrToUINT32' [-Wunused-variable]
9>main.cpp(160,12): warning :       unused variable 'ptrToUINT32' [-Wunused-variable]
9>main.cpp(160,12): warning :            uint32_t* ptrToUINT32 {}; /* When using {} empty braces syntax we are initializing the pointer with the nullptr value. */
9>main.cpp(160,12): warning :
9>main.cpp(166,11): warning :       unused variable 'ptrToINT64' [-Wunused-variable]
9>main.cpp(166,11): warning :            int64_t* ptrToINT64 {}; /* Also initialized with nullptr value when using {} empty braces syntax. */
9>main.cpp(166,11): warning :
9>main.cpp(166,11): warning : 4 warnings generated.
9>Example00.vcxproj -> C:\Projects\RV3\2019\Platforms\Windows\Code\IntroducingMechanismsAndAPIsForMemoryManagement\Ch02\Platforms\Windows\Code\WE - CPP
  \Pointers\Example00 x86\..\..\..\..\Bin\x86\Pointers.Example00.exe
9>Done building project "Example00.vcxproj".
========== Build: 1 succeeded, 0 failed, 0 up-to-date, 9 skipped ==========
```

Figure 2-10. *Result of compilation using the LLVM (clang-cl), with four warnings*

Error List						▾ ▯ ✕
Entire Solution ▾	😣 0 Errors	⚠ 4 Warnings	ⓘ 0 Messages	🔍▾ Build + IntelliSense ▾		Search Error List 🔎▾

⚠	Code	Description	Project	File	Line
⚠ ▲		unused variable 'ptrToUINT64' [-Wunused-variable] unused variable 'ptrToUINT64' [-Wunused-variable] uint64_t* ptrToUINT64 {}; /* Also initialized with nullptr value when using {} empty braces syntax. */	Example00 (Example00 x86\Example00)	main.cpp	164
▷ ⚠		unused variable 'ptrToINT32' [-Wunused-variable]	Example00 (Example00 x86\Example00)	main.cpp	162
▷ ⚠		unused variable 'ptrToUINT32' [-Wunused-variable]	Example00 (Example00 x86\Example00)	main.cpp	160
▷ ⚠		unused variable 'ptrToINT64' [-Wunused-variable]	Example00 (Example00 x86\Example00)	main.cpp	166

Figure 2-11. *Error List window showing the four warnings, all about variables not used*

When changing to the Intel C++ compiler tool set, some basic messages in the Output window indicating success or failure will appear, as shown in Figure 2-12.

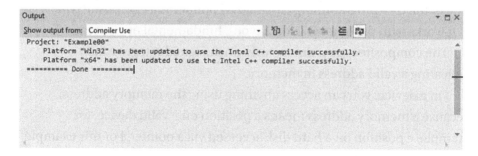

```
Output                                                                            ▾ ▯ ✕
Show output from: Compiler Use                    ▾ | 🎦 | ⇌ | ⏱ ⏱ | 필 | 🗗
Project: "Example00"
    Platform "Win32" has been updated to use the Intel C++ compiler successfully.
    Platform "x64" has been updated to use the Intel C++ compiler successfully.
========== Done ==========
```

Figure 2-12. *Messages indicating success or failure after changing to the Intel C++ compiler*

Figure 2-13 shows the results of the build. When using the default configurations of the MSVC tool set, the warnings shown when using LLVM (clang-cl) are no longer listed.

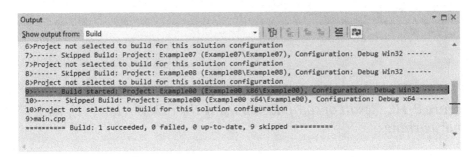

Figure 2-13. *When building using the Intel C++ compiler using default configurations for the MSVC tool set, no warnings are displayed*

A composite type pointer is a formal data type of the C++ programming language. A pointer is a composite type; that is, it works with the other C++ data types, fundamental or custom.

Details About Composite Type Pointers

Like other fundamental types, a composite type pointer is a formal data type of the C++ programming language. A pointer is a composite type; that is, it works with the other C++ data types, fundamental or custom.

The composite type pointer stores an unsigned integer value, indicating a valid address in memory.

On a device, you can access anything using the memory address, because a memory address means a position on a valid device, for example, a position on a hard disk accessed via a pointer. For this example, we will be working with standard RAM.

RAMis organized in bytes; the first byte has the physical address of zero, followed consecutively to the last byte, which has the physical address N-1.

Navigation and manipulation of bytes are done by both hardware and software, but bytes are manipulated as a set (in blocks). Each block of bytes should have a minimum number and a maximum number of bytes, determined by the hardware and supported in its instructions in the Assembly programming language.

A common measurement is the kilogram (kg); 1 gram (g) is equivalent to 1,000 milligrams (mg), 1 kg is equivalent to 1,000 g, and 1,000 g is equivalent to 1,000,000 mg. In a supermarket, ask for 1,000,000 mg of a product and you'll likely get an odd reaction. It is easier and more convenient to request 1 kg of the product.

The same reasoning applies when manipulating blocks of bytes in memory, in this case, RAM. In programming, instead of dealing with individual blocks of bits, the organization happens through blocks of bytes, where each byte is 8 bits. When grouping two bytes, you have a unit of 16 bytes. When grouping four bytes, you have a unit of 32 bits. When grouping 8 bytes, you have a unit of 64 bits each, and so forth. In memory, each byte receives a single unsigned integer value for identifying it, which is its physical address in memory. Well, when it is necessary to access some information in the physical memory, RAM, it is necessary to supply the address. This address in physical memory indicates the location of the byte. The bytes in the sequence of addresses in physical memory can indicate any part of the information; this interpretation depends on how the software is designed to handle these bytes. But it is not the software that accesses the physical memory address; the software only supplies the required memory address, after which the hardware accesses the byte in the address in memory.

When accessing the memory address, containing the desired information, you need to know the total size of that block of information, that is, the total size in bytes, which determines the starting and ending memory addresses. This is the block of bytes is organized, with a start, middle, and end.

Moving bit by bit from start to end is pointless when you know where it starts and where it ends. Moving bit by bit, in addition to being unfeasible in terms of performance, is unfeasible in terms of energy consumption. At this point, you'll learn about one of the most obvious pointer-type properties, which indicates a location.

As indicated by its name, an instance of a composite type pointer points to something, namely, a location. In this case, the location is a valid memory address.

The instance of a composite type pointer has a size. This size is set in bytes, and a block of bytes is treated as a unit. For example, when a variable of a type pointer is defined as 32 bits, it handles groups with four bytes. When a variable of the pointer type is defined with a 64-bit size, it handles eight-byte groups. Moving a memory address to another memory address is performed according to the pointer size. If the pointer has 32 bits of size, the expressions (varPointer + 1), varPointer++, and ++varPointer mean advance four bytes from the current memory address position. The expressions (varPointer - 1), varPointer--, and --varPointer mean go back four bytes from the current memory address position. If the pointer has 64 bits of size, the expressions (varPointer + 1), varPointer++, and ++varPointer mean advance eight bytes from the current memory address position. The expressions (varPointer - 1), varPointer--, and --varPointer mean go back eight bytes from the current memory address position. The manipulation happens in "jumps" of N bytes. This size is determined by the hardware architecture for which the application was designed for, 32-bit or 64-bit. On a 32-bit processor, a pointer is 32 bits. On a 64-bit processor, a pointer is 64 bits. The technical terms *native pointer size* and *natural pointer size* show this size depending on the processor hardware architecture.

Open the solution `<install_folder>\ \IntroducingMechanisms`
`AndAPIsForMemoryManagement\Ch02\Platforms\Windows\Code\`
`WE - CPP\Pointers\Example00 x86\Pointers.sln` and use the project
`Example00.vcxproj`. Listing 2-2 shows the source code.

Listing 2-2. Sample Source Code Compiled for Target x86 (32-Bit)

```
#include <cstdlib>
#include <cstdint>

using namespace std;

void wmain() {

        uint32_t* ptrToUINT32{}; /* When using {} empty
        braces syntax we are initializing the pointer with
        the nullptr value. */

        int32_t* ptrToINT32{}; /* Also initialized with
        nullptr value when using {} empty braces syntax. */

        uint64_t* ptrToUIINT64{}; /* Also initialized with
        nullptr value when using {} empty braces syntax. */

        int64_t* ptrToINT64{}; /* Also initialized with
        nullptr value when using {} empty braces syntax. */

    return;
};
```

Listing 2-2 shows a sequence of pointers for the types uint32_t*,
int32_t*, uint64_t*, and int64_t*.

Figure 2-14 shows the Assembly programming language for the
corresponding C++ code shown in Listing 2-2.

```
uint32_t* ptrToUINT32 {}; /* When using {} empty braces syntax we are initializing the pointer with the nullptr value. */
006E2A28  mov      dword ptr [ptrToUINT32],0

int32_t* ptrToINT32 {}; /* Also initialized with nullptr value when using {} empty braces syntax. */
006E2A2F  mov      dword ptr [ptrToINT32],0

uint64_t* ptrToUIINT64 {}; /* Also initialized with nullptr value when using {} empty braces syntax. */
006E2A36  mov      dword ptr [ptrToUIINT64],0

int64_t* ptrToINT64 {}; /* Also initialized with nullptr value when using {} empty braces syntax. */
006E2A3D  mov      dword ptr [ptrToINT64],0
```

Figure 2-14. *Assembly code shown for the corresponding C++ code to help understand the sequence of instructions*

Figure 2-15 shows the dword fundamental data type of the Assembly programming language. The dword is 32 bits in size, or 4 bytes if you will. The `ptr` keyword of the Assembly programming language indicates that the variable (operand) `ptrToUINT32` is a 32-bit pointer in size. This is done so that the target types pointed to by four pointers are different, but the pointer sizes of all four pointers have dword (doubleword unsigned integer) as a data type and are 32 bits in size.

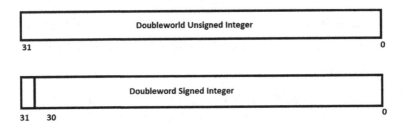

Figure 2-15. *Assembly data types, dword unsigned and signed*

In the Assembly programming language, there are some numeric fundamental data types such as integer and floating-point, as well as the pointer type. In the example, the pointer data type is a dword (32 bits in size).

So, the dword `ptr` is a composite data type, and this is one of the reasons why the pointer is also a composite data type in the C++ and C programming languages.

As shown in Listing 2-2, we are assigning the `nullptr` value to the pointer, or initializing the pointer. In the C programming language, traditionally the `NULL` value is used, which is a macro to the zero value. But in the C++ programming language, you must use the `nullptr` built-in keyword and not the `NULL` macro.

As shown in Figure 2-16, there's a `mov` instruction part in the Assembly programming language. In the source code, the `mov` instruction is assigning the zero value, `nullptr` in the C++ programming language, to the memory address pointed to by the specific pointer variable `ptrToINT32`. The same sequence of instructions and logic of execution is applied to the other pointers, `ptrToUINT32`, `ptrToINT64`, and `ptrToUINT64`.

Open the solution `<install_folder>\ \IntroducingMechanisms AndAPIsForMemoryManagement\Ch02\Platforms\Windows\Code\ WE - CPP\Pointers\Example00 x64\Pointers.sln` and use the project `Example00.vcxproj`. Listing 2-3 shows the source code.

Listing 2-3. Sample Source Code Compiled for Target x64 (64-Bit)

```
#include <cstdlib>
#include <cstdint>

using namespace std;

void wmain() {

        uint32_t* ptrToUINT32{}; /* When using {} empty
        braces syntax we are initializing the pointer with
        the nullptr value. */

        int32_t* ptrToINT32{}; /* Also initialized with
        nullptr value when using {} empty braces syntax. */
```

```
    uint64_t* ptrToUIINT64{}; /* Also initialized with
    nullptr value when using {} empty braces syntax. */

    int64_t* ptrToINT64{}; /* Also initialized with
    nullptr value when using {} empty braces syntax. */

  return;
}
```

```
  uint32_t* ptrToUINT32 {}; /* When using {} empty braces syntax we are initializing the pointer with the nullptr value. */ ◄|
◇ 00007FF7267B2CFF  mov      qword ptr [ptrToUINT32],0

  int32_t* ptrToINT32 {}; /* Also initialized with nullptr value when using {} empty braces syntax. */
  00007FF7267B2D07  mov      qword ptr [ptrToINT32],0

  uint64_t* ptrToUIINT64 {}; /* Also initialized with nullptr value when using {} empty braces syntax. */
  00007FF7267B2D0F  mov      qword ptr [ptrToUIINT64],0

  int64_t* ptrToINT64 {}; /* Also initialized with nullptr value when using {} empty braces syntax. */
  00007FF7267B2D17  mov      qword ptr [ptrToINT64],0
```

Figure 2-16. *Assembly source code with the C++ source code to help understand the sequence of instructions*

Listing 2-3 shows a sequence of pointers for the types uint32_t*, int32_t*, uint64_t*, and int64_t*. This time the software is compiled to target x64 (64-bit) instead of x86 (32-bit).

Figure 2-16 shows the sequence in the Assembly programming language for the corresponding sequence in C++ shown in Listing 2-3.

Figure 2-17 shows the qword fundamental data type of the Assembly programming language. The qword is 64 bits in size, or 8 bytes if you will. The ptr keyword of the Assembly programming language indicates that the variable (operand) ptrToUINT64 is a 64-bit pointer in size. This is done so that the target types pointed to by the four pointers are different, but the pointer sizes of all four pointers have qword (quadword unsigned integer) as the data type and are 64 bits in size.

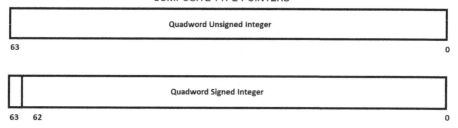

Figure 2-17. *Assembly data types, qword unsigned and signed*

In the Assembly programming language, there are numeric fundamental data types such as integer and floating-point; in addition, there is the pointer type. In this example, the pointer data type is a qword that is 64 bits in size.

So, the qword ptr is a composite data type, and this is one of the reasons why the pointer is also a composite data type in the C++ and C programming languages.

In Listing 2-3, we are assigning the nullptr value to the pointer, or initializing the pointer. In the C programming language, traditionally we have used the NULL value, which is a macro to the zero value. But in the C++ programming language, you must use the nullptr built-in keyword and not the NULL macro.

Also as shown in Listing 2-3, we have the mov instruction part of the Assembly programming language. In this source code, the mov instruction is assigning the zero value, projected as nullptr in the C++ programming language, to the memory address pointed to by the specific pointer variable ptrToINT64. The same sequence of instructions and logic of execution is applied to the other pointers, ptrToUINT32, ptrToINT64, and ptrToUINT64.

33

CHAPTER 3

Working with Smart Pointers: unique_ptr

In this chapter, you'll learn about memory management using smart pointers in the C++ programming language.

Acronyms

This chapter uses the following acronyms:

- Microsoft Foundation Classes (MFC)

- Run-Time Type Information (RTTI)

Pointers

Chapter 2 gave you an overview of composite type pointers, introducing some concepts and showing a practical use of a composite type pointer.

In this chapter, you will be working with raw pointers and will start working with smart pointers. Specifically, you will learn about unique_ptr, and in Chapter 4 you will learn about the shared_ptr and weak_ptr smart pointers.

© Roger Villela 2020
R. Villela, *Introducing Mechanisms and APIs for Memory Management*,
https://doi.org/10.1007/978-1-4842-5416-5_3

As discussed in Chapter 1, the sample source projects have been tested on the following C++ platform tool sets of Microsoft Visual C++ whenever possible. Check the GitHub repository to download the sample projects and explanations about the configurations for the platform tool set in each sample project when required.

- By default all sample projects using the Microsoft Visual C++ 2019 platform tool set configured to the option Visual Studio 2019 (v142)

- Also, when possible, tested with the following:

  - Microsoft Visual C++ 2019 platform tool set configured to the option Visual Studio 2017 (v141)

  - Microsoft Visual C++ 2019 platform tool set configured to the option Visual Studio 2015 (v140)

  - Microsoft Visual C++ 2019 platform tool set configured to the option Visual Studio 2010 (v100)

  - Microsoft Visual C++ 2019 platform tool set configured to the option LLVM (clang-cl)

  - Microsoft Visual C++ 2019 platform tool set configured to the option Intel C++ Compiler 19.0

There's one solution named `Pointers` and various sample projects within the solution `Pointers` named `Example00`, `Example01`, `Example02`, and so on.

Using Raw Pointers

Open the solution `Pointers` in `<install folder>\Platforms\Windows\Code\Ch03\`. Go to the project `Example00 x64\Example00` or `Example x86\Example00`, and open the `main.cpp` source code file. Both of these files have the same source code; the difference is in the default size of the pointer because of the target platform, x86 for 32-bit and x64 for 64-bit.

Listing 3-1 shows four raw pointers named ptrToUINT32, ptrToINT32, ptrToUINT64, and ptrToINT64 for the respective types uint32_t, int32_t, uint64_t, and int64_t.

In addition, there's a raw pointer named rPerson that points to an instance of class Person.

The pointers in Listing 3-1 are created directly using the indirection (∗) operator and called *raw pointers*. You are responsible for managing practically every operation and memory allocation until the memory is released.

On a basic code level, this does not sound complicated, but with hundreds of lines of code, severe errors can and do occur.

One of the principles of smart pointers is to avoid part of the complexity of managing certain tasks, such as memory allocation and release.

Listing 3-1. Raw Pointers

```
#include <cstdio>
#include <cstdlib>
#include <cstdint>
#include <cwchar>
#include <typeinfo>
#include <memory>

#include <conio.h>
#include <afx.h>

using namespace std;

void Pause( bool finish = false ) {

        constexpr wchar_t* _finishMessage { L"Press <ENTER> to
        finish..." };
        constexpr wchar_t* _pauseMessage { L"Press <ENTER> to
        continue..." };
```

```
        _cwprintf_s( L"\n\n%s\n\n", !finish ? _pauseMessage :
        _finishMessage );

        _getwchar_nolock();

        return;
};
wchar_t* YesNo( bool confirmed ) {

        return ( confirmed ? L"yes" : L"no" );

};
class Person : public CObject {};

class Employee : public Person {};

void wmain() {

        uint32_t* ptrToUINT32 {}; /* When using {} empty braces
        syntax we are initializing the pointer with the nullptr
        value. */

        int32_t* ptrToINT32 {}; /* Also initialized with nullptr
        value when using {} empty braces syntax. */

        uint64_t* ptrToUINT64 {}; /* Also initialized with
        nullptr value when using {} empty braces syntax. */

        int64_t* ptrToINT64 {}; /* Also initialized with nullptr
        value when using {} empty braces syntax. */

        _cwprintf_s( L"\n\nUsing RAW POINTERS\n\n" );

        Person* rPerson{ new Person() };

        const type_info& personInfo { typeid( rPerson ) };
```

```
bool ancestor { ( typeid( CObject ).
before( personInfo ) ) };

_cwprintf_s( L"Human-readable name: %S\n\nUndecoretad
name: %S\n\nCObject is an ancestor?: %s\n\nPerson is a
descendent?: %s", personInfo.name(), personInfo.raw_
name(), YesNo( ancestor ), YesNo( ancestor ) );

delete rPerson; rPerson = nullptr;
return;
};
```

Using Smart Pointers

Smart pointers are classes and functions defined in specific header files in the std namespace, and to use of any of them, you need to include at least one header file.

Note   Include the header file <memory> or <memory.h>.

There are different ways to create instances of a target type using instances of the unique_ptr smart pointer.

It is not necessary to use the new operator to create an instance of a unique_ptr smart pointer, nor is it necessary to use the delete operator to release the memory allocated for the unique_ptr smart pointer and the target type, such as class Person in the code shown in Listing 3-2. Using the delete operator can cause unpredictable results.

In addition, it is not necessary to use the indirection (*) operator on a variable of type unique_ptr or on the target type passed as an argument value to the template class of a unique_ptr smart pointer.

A smart pointer is automatically deallocated when falling out of scope, but it is a fundamental practice when using raw pointers to always assign a nullptr to the smart pointer when it is no longer in use.

Open the solution Pointers in <install folder>\Platforms\ Windows\Code\Ch03\. Go to the project Example01 and open the main.cpp source code file.

Listing 3-2. Using the unique_ptr Smart Pointer

```cpp
#include <cstdlib>
#include <cstdint>

#include <memory>

#include <afx.h>

using namespace std;

void Pause( bool finish = false ) {

        constexpr wchar_t* _finishMessage { L"Press <ENTER> for
        finish..." };
        constexpr wchar_t* _pauseMessage { L"Press <ENTER> for
        continue..." };

        _cwprintf_s( L"\n\n%s\n\n", !finish ? _pauseMessage :
        _finishMessage );

        _getwchar_nolock();

        return;
};

class Person : public CObject {
};
```

```
void wmain() {

        uint32_t* ptrToUINT32 {};

        int32_t* ptrToINT32 {};

        uint64_t* ptrToUIINT64 {}

        int64_t* ptrToINT64 {};

        Person* pPerson{ new Person() };

        delete pPerson; pPerson = nullptr;

        unique_ptr<Person> pPerson { new Person() };

        pPerson = nullptr;

        Pause( true );

        return;
};
```

Using the make_unique Template Function

Another way to create an instance of unique_ptr and an instance of the target type is to use the make_unique template function. Internally, make_unique creates an instance of unique_ptr and an instance of the target type, as shown in Figure 3-1.

The definition of the make_unique template function can be seen on the following page of Microsoft official documentation:

https://docs.microsoft.com/en-us/cpp/standard-library/memory-functions?view=vs-2019#make_unique

The make_unique and unique_ptr pointers are based on template technology.

```cpp
// make_unique<T>
template <class T, class... Types>
   unique_ptr<T> make_unique(Types&&... Args)
   {
       return (unique_ptr<T>(new T(forward<Types>(Args)...)));
   }

// make_unique<T[]>
template <class T>
   make_unique(size_t Size)
   {
       return (unique_ptr<T>(new Elem[Size]()));
   }

// make_unique<T[N]> disallowed
template <class T, class... Types>
   typename enable_if<extent<T>::value != 0, void>::type make_unique(Types&&...) = delete;
```

Figure 3-1. *Definition of the make_unique template function*

Open the solution `Pointers` in `<install folder>\Platforms\`
`Windows\Code\Ch03\`. Go to the project `Example02` and open the `main.cpp`
source code file. Listing 3-3 shows how to use `make_unique` to create an
instance of `unique_ptr`.

Listing 3-3. Using make_unique to Create an Instance of unique_ptr

```cpp
#include <cstdlib>
#include <cstdint>
#include <string>
#include <memory>

#include <afx.h>

using namespace std;

void Pause( bool finish = false ) {
```

```
        constexpr wchar_t* _finishMessage { L"Press <ENTER> to
        finish..." };
        constexpr wchar_t* _pauseMessage { L"Press <ENTER> to
        continue..." };

        _cwprintf_s( L"\n\n%s\n\n", !finish ? _pauseMessage :
        _finishMessage );

        _getwchar_nolock();

        return;
};

class Person : public CObject {};

void Scenario00() {

        unique_ptr<Person> pPerson { new Person() };

        pPerson = nullptr;

        return;
};

void Scenario01() {

        unique_ptr<Person> pPerson { make_unique<Person>() };

        pPerson = nullptr;

        return;
};

void wmain() {

        Scenario00();
        Pause()
```

```
        Scenario01();
        Pause();

        return;
};
```

Characteristics of unique_ptr

A smart pointer cannot be shared, which is one notable characteristic of a
unique_ptr<T>.

Listing 3-4 shows that an instance of unique_ptr cannot be assigned
another variable of type unique_ptr. Applying the concepts of not being
shared or copied, you can only move the instance, meaning you copy the
state for the new instance, not the source instance itself.

Listing 3-4. A unique_ptr Cannot Be Shared

```
#include <cstdlib>
#include <cstdint>
#include <string>
#include <memory>

#include <afx.h>

using namespace std;

void Pause( bool finish = false ) {

        constexpr wchar_t* _finishMessage { L"Press <ENTER> for
        finish..." };
        constexpr wchar_t* _pauseMessage { L"Press <ENTER> for
        continue..." };

        _cwprintf_s( L"\n\n%s\n\n", !finish ? _pauseMessage :
        _finishMessage );
```

```cpp
        _getwchar_nolock();

        return;
};

class Person : public CObject {
};

void Scenario02() {
    Person* rPersonOne{ new Person() };
    Person* rPersonTwo{};
    /* Person* rPersonTwo{ rPersonOne }; */

    delete rPersonOne, rPersonTwo = nullptr, rPersonOne =
    nullptr;

    pPersonOne = nullptr, pPersonTwo = nullptr;

    unique_ptr<Person> pPersonOne{ make_unique<Person>()};
    unique_ptr<Person> pPersonTwo{};
    /* unique_ptr<Person> pPersonTwo{ PersonOne }; */

    rPersonTwo = rPersonOne;

    //pPersonTwo = pPersonOne;
    return;
};
```

As shown in Figure 3-2, using raw pointers, it's possible to have two pointers pointing to the same instance of an object.

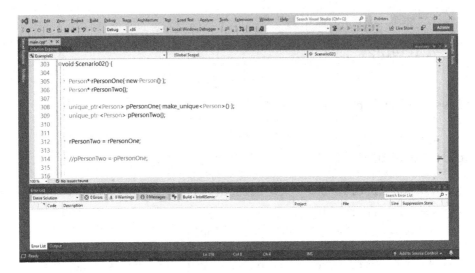

Figure 3-2. *Using raw pointers to share an instance of a target object*

Figure 3-3 shows the comments removed from the line of code with the assignment between two `unique_ptr` instances; note that the error appears even before the building.

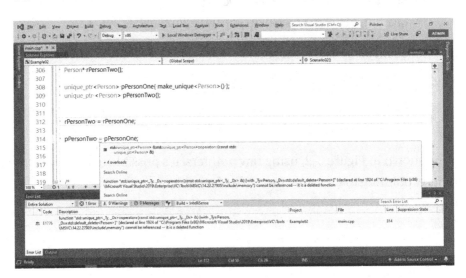

Figure 3-3. *Error occurring before building*

This is because the default operator (=) assignment and the signature for the assignment of argument value `nullptr` have both been overridden and overloaded, and then two typical signatures were deleted from the class `unique_ptr`, as shown in Figure 3-4. Highlighted are two lines of code; the first is a copy constructor that was deleted, and the second is a default implementation for the assignment (=) operator that was also deleted.

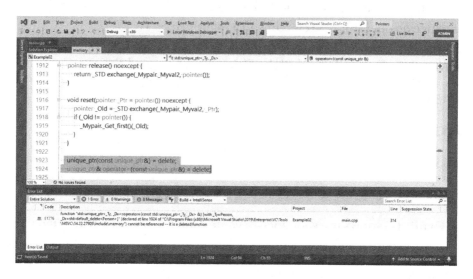

Figure 3-4. *Default assignment operator deleted, and a copy constructor also deleted*

As shown in Listing 3-5, the constant `unique_ptr&` is the left-side assignment of the expression using the assignment operator and the left operand that will receive the value that was supplied on the right side of expression.

The left side of an expression with the assignment is called an *lvalue*. When a type precedes the operator &, it is working with an lvalue operator in an expression.

The code shown in Listing 3-5 will help you understand the concepts of lvalue and rvalue.

First, a variable X is declared and defined with a value.

47

Second, we have an lvalue reference uint32_t& to the X variable.

Third, we have a variable named L that receives the value pointed to by the Lvalue reference Y.

Fourth, we have a rvalue reference uint32_t&& that points to an expression for which the compiler creates a temporary variable storing the result of the expression. The rvalue reference uint32_t&& points to this temporary variable automatically created by the compiler. An rvalue reference && operator is a reference to a reference.

Listing 3-5. Left-Side and Right-Side Operators and Expressions

```
uint32_t X{ 90 };
```

uint32_t& X{ Y };

```
uint32_t L{ Y };
```

```
uint32_t&& Z{ ( Y * L ) };
```

Figure 3-5 shows the sequence of values and the results as expected.

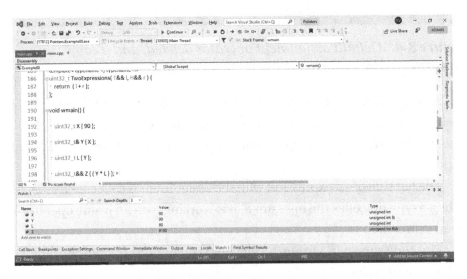

Figure 3-5. *Left side and right side of an expression*

Shown in Figure 3-5 is the right side of an expression, which is acting as a source of data; this is called an *rvalue*. When a type precedes the operator &&, it is acting as an rvalue operator, as in the expression uint32_t&& X{ (Y * 100)};.

With this powerful mechanism for capturing contextual values (that is, from a specific side of an expression, either lvalue or rvalue), we can create things like what's shown in Listing 3-6. This is a template function that receives expressions as syntactic paths to one or more variables.

Listing 3-6. Function Tempate Receiving Two Expressions as Argument Values

```
template< typename T, typename H>
uint32_t TwoExpressions( T&& l, H&& r ) {
      return ( l + r );
};

uint32_t index { 20 };

index =  TwoExpressions<uint32_t, uint32_t>( ( index * 10 ), (
index * 30 ) ) ;
```

The unique_ptr pPersonTwo is the left side of the expression waiting to receive a copy of the pointer to the instance of unique_ptr pPersonOne. This is the signature and implementation that were deleted for the assignment operator, as shown in Listing 3-7.

Listing 3-7. Excerpt of Code for the Two Signatures and Implementations of Copy Constructor and Assignment Operator, Both Deleted

```
unique_ptr( const unique_ptr&) = delete;
unique_ptr& operator=(const unique_ptr&) = delete;
```

pPersonOne is the left side of the expression that is expecting to receive the nullptr value, but this will not happen because the second signature and implementation were also deleted, as shown in Listing 3-8.

Listing 3-8. Left-Side Assignments of Expressions Using the Assignment Operator

```
#include <cstdint>
#include <cstdlib>
#include <string>
#include <memory>

/* MFC */

#include <afx.h>

using namespace std;

    void Pause( bool finish = false ) {

        constexpr wchar_t* _finishMessage { L"Press <ENTER>
        for finish..." };
        constexpr wchar_t* _pauseMessage { L"Press <ENTER>
        for continue..."
        };

        _cwprintf_s( L"\n\n%s\n\n", !finish ? _pauseMessage
        : _finishMessage
        );

        _getwchar_nolock();

        return;
    };
class Person : CObject {
};
```

```
void Scenario02() {

unique_ptr<Person> pPersonOne{ make_unique<Person()> };
unique_ptr<Person> pPersonTwo{};

Person* rPersonOne{ new Person() };
Person* rPersonTwo{};

rPersonTwo = rPersonOne;

pPersonTwo = pPersonOne;

delete rPersonOne, rPersonTwo = nullptr, rPersonOne = nullptr;

pPersonOne = nullptr, pPersonTwo = nullptr;

return;

};

void wmain() {

        Scenario02();
      Pause( true );

        return;
};
```

Open the header file <memory> and go to the unique_ptr class and definition of the assignment operator marked as deleted, as shown in Figure 3-6.

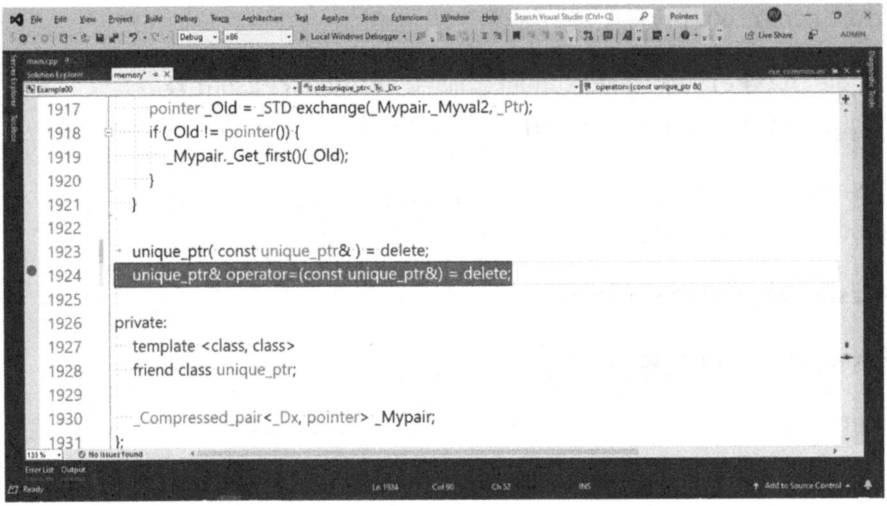

Figure 3-6. *Before removing the delete keyword from a default implementation for the assignment operator*

We can remove the `delete` keyword from the template functions and instead provide a custom implementation (Figure 3-7). This is shown in Listing 3-9.

Listing 3-9. Custom Implementations for Assignment Operator That Was Deleted

```
unique_ptr& operator=(const unique_ptr&) {
        return *this;
    };
```

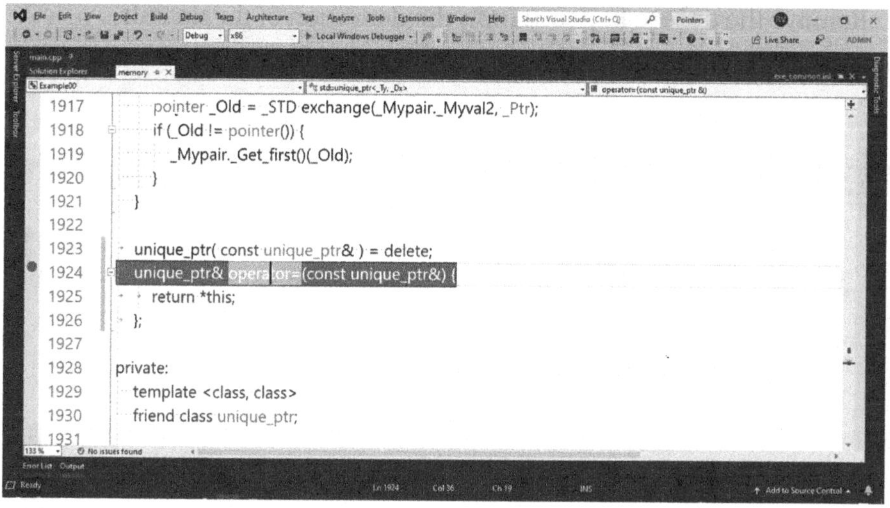

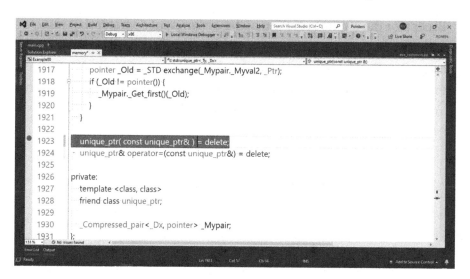

Figure 3-7. *After removing the delete keyword from a default implementation for the assignment operator*

Open the header file <memory> and go to the unique_ptr class and definition of constructor marked as deleted, as shown in Figure 3-8.

Figure 3-8. *Before removing the delete keyword from a default implementation for a constructor member function*

Remove the `delete` keyword from the definition of the default constructor for the `unique_ptr` class, as shown in Figure 3-9.

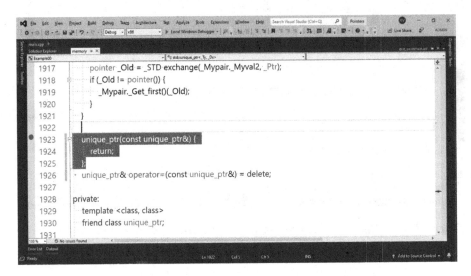

Figure 3-9. *After removing the delete keyword from a default implementation for a constructor member function*

Except for the implementation of the assignment operator that was deleted, we have various implementations overridden and overloaded for the assignment operator.

Figure 3-10 shows two of these implementations that were overridden and overloaded for the assignment operator.

```
1861              is_convertible<typename unique_ptr<_Ty2, _Dx2>::pointer, pointer>>,
1862          int> = 0>
1863   unique_ptr& operator=(unique_ptr<_Ty2, _Dx2>&& _Right) noexcept {
1864       reset(_Right.release());
1865       _Mypair._Get_first() = _STD forward<_Dx2>(_Right._Mypair._Get_first());
1866       return *this;
1867   }
1868
1869   unique_ptr& operator=(unique_ptr&& _Right) noexcept {
1870       if (this != _STD addressof(_Right)) {
1871           reset(_Right.release());
1872           _Mypair._Get_first() = _STD forward<_Dx>(_Right._Mypair._Get_first());
1873       }
1874       return *this;
1875   }
```

Figure 3-10. *Overridden and overloaded implementations for the assignment operator*

Listing 3-10 shows the noexcept keyword introduced with the C++11 standard for suffixing a function for the creation of a noexcept expression with the purpose of defining an exception specification.

Listing 3-10. Overridden and Overloaded Implementations for the Assignment Operator

```
unique_ptr& operator=(unique_ptr<_Ty2, _Dx2>&& _Right)
noexcept {
                    reset(_Right.release());
    _Mypair._Get_first() = ::std:: forward<_Dx2>(_Right._
    Mypair._Get_first());
    return *this;
}
```

```
unique_ptr& operator=(unique_ptr&& _Right) noexcept {
    if (this != ::std::addressof(_Right)) {
                            reset(_Right.release());
        _Mypair._Get_first() = ::std:: forward<_Dx>(_
        Right._Mypair._Get_first());
    }
    return *this;
}
```

One unique_ptr cannot be copied to another unique_ptr. The concept of copying a unique_ptr is for assigning more than one instance of unique_ptr that points to the same instance of unique_ptr. A copy constructor is required, but the copy constructor was deleted from the implementation of the unique_ptr template class.

One unique_ptr cannot be passed by value to a function, using a template or not, and cannot be used in any C++ Standard Library algorithm that requires copies to be made.

A unique_ptr can only be moved; this means that the ownership of the memory resource is transferred to another unique_ptr, and the original unique_ptr no longer owns it.

For now, that's all there is to know about unique_ptr. The discussion will continue in Chapter 4, which covers move semantics and using unique_ptr with arrays, as well as another two smart pointers, shared_ptr and weak_ptr.

Do's

- Do adopt smart pointers when possible.

- Do use unique_ptr for scenarios where the pointers are not shared.

- Do avoid breaking the rules of standard C++ for smart pointers, such as implementing custom code for `<memory>` and `unique_ptr` to copy operations between instances of `unique_ptr`.

- For advanced code, when using raw pointers, do test the code properly to reduce the risk of security problems.

- For custom code for the smart pointers `unique_ptr`, `shared_ptr`, and `weak_ptr`, do copy the necessary documents and source code and create an independent version for a binary distribution, not with source code.

- Do learn about programming with templates.

- Do learn about C++ RTTI.

- Do learn about OOP.

- Do learn about algorithms.

Don'ts

- Don't try to force nonstandard behaviors defined by C++ Standard, such as copy operations for the `unique_ptr` smart pointer inside the original source code.

- Don't try to change the purpose of the smart pointers, such as implementing the natural behaviors of `unique_ptr` in `shared_ptr` or `weak_ptr`, or vice versa.

- Don't create complex code just because of the "personal ego." Create a simple and objective code implementation.

- Don't update the original source code of C++ Standard, except when documented by the committee or by internal documentation with an objective and formal purpose.

- Don't make changes just because you can.

- Don't make changes without understanding the fundamentals of programming with templates, RTTI, OOP, and algorithms.

CHAPTER 4

Working with Smart Pointers: unique_ptr, shared_ptr, and weak_ptr

In this chapter, you'll learn more about memory management using the smart pointers unique_ptr, shared_ptr, and weak_ptr.

Pointers Review

Chapter 3 gave you an overview of the composite type pointer, introducing some concepts and presenting a practical use of a composite type pointer. In Chapter 3 you also started to work with raw pointers and with smart pointers, specifically with unique_ptr.

In this chapter, you will learn about more specific features of unique_ptr and also learn about shared_ptr and weak_ptr.

© Roger Villela 2020
R. Villela, *Introducing Mechanisms and APIs for Memory Management*,
https://doi.org/10.1007/978-1-4842-5416-5_4

As we talked about in previous chapters, the sample source projects are provided on these tool sets through Microsoft Visual 2019:

- All sample projects using the Microsoft Visual Studio 2019 tool set as the default for building.

- When possible, the sample projects are also compiled via Microsoft Visual Studio 2019 using the tool sets for the following:

  - Microsoft Visual Studio 2017

  - Microsoft Visual Studio 2015

  - Microsoft Visual Studio 2010

For this chapter we have one solution named `Smart_Pointers` and one sample project within this solution named `Example00`.

More About Using Smart Pointers

As mentioned in Chapter 3, smart pointers are template-based classes and functions defined in header files in the `std` namespace. When using smart pointers, we need to include at least one header file.

Important   Include the header file `<memory>` or `<memory.h>`.

When using smart pointers, it is not necessary to use the `new` operator to create an instance of a smart pointer. Also, it is not necessary to use the `delete` operator to release the memory allocated for the smart pointer and the target type, such as the class `Person` in the code shown in Listing 4-1. Using the `delete` operator can even cause unpredictable results.

Also, we do not need to use the indirection (*) operator on a variable of a smart pointer type.

It is a fundamental practice when using raw pointers to always assign a `nullptr` once the pointer is no longer in use and still in scope. Once a smart pointer is out of scope, the smart pointer and the resource owned by it are automatically destroyed, so there's no need to assign a `nullptr` value.

Using the make_shared Template Function

Like with `unique_ptr` that uses the `make_unique` template function, it is recommended you use the `std::make_shared` template function to create an instance of `std::shared_ptr`. Internally, `std::make_shared` creates an instance of the target resource using an overridden implementation of the `new` operator.

Listing 4-1 uses `std::make_shared` instead of the global operator `::new` for memory allocation of the target resource owned by the smart pointer `shared_ptr`. Internally, the function `std::make_shared` uses the global operator `::new` to create the instance of the target resource. When the instance of a smart pointer is out of scope or `nullptr` is explicitly assigned for an instance of `std::shared_ptr`, internally the `delete` operator is called, and the instance of resource is destroyed from memory. The smart pointer itself is destroyed only when out of scope. When `nullptr` is assigned, the smart pointer is not destroyed; only the internal resource is destroyed from memory.

As illustrated by Figure 4-1, you can look at the declaration of the `make_shared` template function.

The Microsoft official documentation discusses the make_shared template-based function on this page:

https://docs.microsoft.com/en-us/cpp/standard-library/memory-functions?view=vs-2019#make_shared

The make_shared and shared_ptr template functions are based on C++ template technology.

```cpp
C++                                                              ⧉ Copy

template <class T, class... Args>
shared_ptr<T> make_shared(
    Args&&... args);
```

Figure 4-1. *Declaration of the make_shared template function*

Open the solution Smart_Pointers in <install folder>\Platforms\Windows\Code\Ch04\Smart_Pointers. Go to the project Example00, open the main.cpp source code file, and go to the Scenario03 function, as shown in Listing 4-1.

Listing 4-1. Using std::make_shared to Create a New Instance of shared_ptr and the Resource

```
#pragma region Header Files

#include <cstdlib>
#include <cstdint>
#include <cstdio>
#include <memory>
#include <typeinfo>
#include <cwchar>

#include <conio.h>

/* MFC */
#include <afx.h>
```

```cpp
/* RVJ */
#include <Utils.h>

#pragma endregion

#pragma region Namespaces

using namespace std;

#pragma endregion

#pragma region Class Person

class Person : public CObject {
public:
        Person() {

                _cwprintf_s( L"Constructor of Person.\n\n" );

        };
        ~Person() {

                _cwprintf_s( L"Destructor of Person.\n\n" );

        };
public:

        /* Potential for cyclic pointers!!! This is not
        recommended. */
        Person* another {};

};

#pragma endregion

#pragma region Scenario03 - shared_ptr Smart Pointer - Learning
about owner concept.
```

```
void Scenario03() {

        shared_ptr<Person> spPerson { make_shared<Person>() };
        // Owner
        shared_ptr<Person> spPerson00 { spPerson }; // Not
        owner, just a new reference.
        shared_ptr<Person> spPerson01 { make_shared<Person>() };
        // Owner
        shared_ptr<Person> spPerson02{ new Person() }; // Owner

        _cwprintf_s( L"Number of shared_ptr that points to the
        same resource: %d\n\n", spPerson.use_count() );

        if ( const wchar_t* yes_or_no = YesOrNo( spPerson01.
        owner_before( spPerson ) ) ) {

                _cwprintf_s( L"Owner before on hierarchy: %s",
                yes_or_no );

        };

        Pause();
        _flushall();
        _wsystem( L"cls" );

        return;
};

#pragma endregion
```

The Scenario03 function shows how to create an instance of a shared_ptr using the std::make_shared template function and using the overridden implementation of the new operator. Both the std::make_shared template function and the overridden implementation of the new operator return an instance of std::shared_ptr, which is filled with values for the instance of the new target resource and with internal data used by the smart pointer for managing the owned resource.

After assigning a `nullptr` to the variable of a smart pointer data type, the instance of the smart pointer is *not* destroyed from memory. The internal data values are reset, meaning that the internally stored resource is destroyed from memory, and the smart pointer can be used again, receiving a new resource via the assignment operator (that is, a new target object for keeping and owning).

The smart pointer is destroyed only when out of scope, which happens automatically.

Ownership, Scope, and Reference Counting

On the object-oriented programming (OOP) side, the source object instance does not need to be destroyed after a copy operation. This is done only if this is something defined by the application logic, that is, by the algorithm implemented for the copy operation in the application.

A smart pointer is a manager of the lifetime of a new object (in the abstract sense), from creation until destruction.

Between these two fundamental points, creation and destruction, we have a set of functionality that helps us with the use of smart pointers.

Listing 4-2 shows a sequence of eight sample functions, named `Scenario00...Scenario07`, with respective comments about the behaviors of raw pointers, `unique_ptr`, and smart pointers in each. We describe each sample function in the sections that follow. Listing 4-2 shows the full source code for project `Example00`.

Listing 4-2. Full Source Code for Project Example00

```
#ifdef __INTEL_COMPILER
// Disable warning for wmain() not returning an integer value.
#pragma warning(  disable : 1079 )
#else
```

```cpp
// Disable warning for wmain() not returning an integer value.
#pragma warning(  disable : 4326 )

#endif

#pragma region Header Files

#include <cstdlib>
#include <cstdint>
#include <cstdio>
#include <memory>
#include <typeinfo>
#include <cwchar>

#include <conio.h>

/* MFC */
#include <afx.h>

/* RVJ */
#include <Utils.h>

#pragma endregion

#pragma region Namespaces

using namespace std;

#pragma endregion

#pragma region Class Person

class Person : public CObject {
public:
        Person() {

                _cwprintf_s( L"Constructor of Person.\n\n" );

        };
```

```
        ~Person() {

                _cwprintf_s( L"Destructor of Person.\n\n" );

        };
public:

        /* Potential for cyclic pointers!!! This is not
        recommended. */
        Person* another {};

};

#pragma endregion

#pragma region Scenario 00 - RAW Pointers

void Scenario00() {

        Person* rPerson { new Person() };
        Person* rPerson00 { rPerson };
        Person* rPerson01 { rPerson };
        Person* rPerson02 { rPerson };

        uint8_t* rUINT8 { new uint8_t( 0x0000 ) };
        uint8_t* rUINT8_00 { rUINT8 };

        uint16_t* rUINT16 { new uint16_t( 0xA000 ) };
        uint16_t* rUINT16_00 { rUINT16 };

        uint32_t* rUINT32 { new uint32_t( 0xC000 ) };
        uint32_t* rUINT32_00 { rUINT32 };

        uint64_t* rUINT64 { new uint64_t( 0xF000 ) };
        uint64_t* rUINT64_00 { rUINT64 };

        delete rUINT64_00;
        delete rUINT32_00;
```

```
        delete rUINT16_00;
        delete rUINT8_00;
        delete rPerson00;

        rUINT64 = nullptr;
        rUINT64_00 = nullptr;
        rUINT32 = nullptr;
        rUINT32_00 = nullptr;
        rUINT16 = nullptr;
        rUINT16_00 = nullptr;
        rUINT8 = nullptr;
        rUINT8_00 = nullptr;
        rPerson = nullptr;
        rPerson00 = nullptr;
        rPerson01 = nullptr;
        rPerson02 = nullptr;

        Pause();
        _flushall();
        _wsystem( L"cls" );

        return;
};

#pragma endregion

#pragma region Scenario01 - unique_ptr Smart Pointer - Using
multiple scopes

void Scenario01() {

    {

            unique_ptr<Person> upPerson { make_
            unique<Person>() };

    };
```

```cpp
        // Out of scope is destroyed from memory.

        Pause();
        _flushall();
        _wsystem( L"cls" );

        return;
};

#pragma endregion

#pragma region Scenario02 - unique_ptr Smart Pointer - multiple
references.

/* Two instances of unique_ptr cannot points to the same
instance. */
void Scenario02() {

        {

                unique_ptr<Person> upPerson { make_
                unique<Person>() };
                /* unique_ptr<Person> upPerson00 { upPerson }; */

        };

        // Out of scope, the smart pointer is destroyed from
        memory.

        Pause();
        _flushall();
        _wsystem( L"cls" );

        return;
};
```

```cpp
#pragma endregion

#pragma region Scenario03 - shared_ptr Smart Pointer - Learning
about owner concept.

void Scenario03() {

        shared_ptr<Person> spPerson { make_shared<Person>() };
        // Owner
        shared_ptr<Person> spPerson00 { spPerson }; // Not
        owner, just a new reference.
        shared_ptr<Person> spPerson01 { make_shared<Person>() };
        // Owner
        shared_ptr<Person> spPerson02 { new Person() }; // Owner

        _cwprintf_s( L"Number of shared_ptr that points to the
        same resource: %d\n\n", spPerson.use_count() );

        /*if ( const wchar_t* yes_or_no = YesOrNo( spPerson01.
        owner_before( spPerson ) ) ) {

                _cwprintf_s( L"Owner before on hierarchy:
                %s\n\n", yes_or_no );

        };*/

        Pause();
        _flushall();
        _wsystem( L"cls" );

        return;
};

#pragma endregion

#pragma region Scenario04 - shared_ptr Smart Pointer - Learning
about reference counting concept.
```

```
void Scenario04() {

    shared_ptr<Person> spPerson { make_shared<Person>() };
    // Owner
    shared_ptr<Person> spPerson01 { make_shared<Person>() };
    // Owner

    long numberOfReferencesFirst { spPerson.use_count() };
    long numberOfReferencesSecond { spPerson01.use_count() };

    _cwprintf_s( L"Number of shared_ptrs that point for the
    spPerson: %d\n\n", numberOfReferencesFirst );

// Not owner, just a new reference.
    shared_ptr<Person> spPerson00 { spPerson };

    numberOfReferencesFirst = spPerson00.use_count();

    _cwprintf_s( L"Number of shared_ptrs that point for the
    spPerson: %d\n\n", numberOfReferencesFirst );

    _cwprintf_s( L"Number of shared_ptrs that point for the
    spPerson01: %d\n\n", numberOfReferencesSecond );

    /* Minus one reference to spPerson.  */
    spPerson00 = nullptr;
    --numberOfReferencesFirst;

    _cwprintf_s( L"Number of shared_ptrs that point for the
    spPerson: %d\n\n", numberOfReferencesFirst );

    /* Minus one reference to spPerson.  */
    spPerson = nullptr;
    --numberOfReferencesFirst;

    _cwprintf_s( L"Number of shared_ptrs that point for the
    spPerson: %d\n\n", numberOfReferencesFirst );
```

```cpp
        _cwprintf_s( L"Number of shared_ptrs that point for the
        spPerson01: %d\n\n", numberOfReferencesSecond );

        spPerson01 = nullptr;
        --numberOfReferencesSecond;

        _cwprintf_s( L"Number of shared_ptrs that point for the
        spPerson01: %d\n\n", numberOfReferencesSecond );

        Pause();
        _flushall();
        _wsystem( L"cls" );

        return;
};

#pragma endregion

#pragma region Scenario05 - shared_ptr Smart Pointer - Learning
about reference counting using scope.

void Scenario05() {

        shared_ptr<Person> spPerson { make_shared<Person>() };
        // Owner

        long numberOfReferencesFirst { spPerson.use_count() };
        long numberOfReferencesSecond {};

        _cwprintf_s( L"Number of shared_ptrs that point for the
        spPerson: %d\n\n", numberOfReferencesFirst );

        {

                /* Open scope. More one reference for spPerson. */
                shared_ptr<Person> spPerson00 { spPerson }; //
                Not owner, just a new reference.
```

```
        numberOfReferencesFirst = spPerson.use_count();

        _cwprintf_s( L"Number of shared_ptrs that point
        for spPerson: %d\n\n", numberOfReferencesFirst );

}

/*  Closed scope. Minus  one reference for spPerson. */
numberOfReferencesFirst = spPerson.use_count();

_cwprintf_s( L"Number of shared_ptrs that point for
spPerson: %d\n\n", numberOfReferencesFirst );

{

        shared_ptr<Person> spPerson01 { make_
        shared<Person>() }; // Owner

        numberOfReferencesSecond = spPerson01.use_
        count();

        _cwprintf_s( L"Number of shared_ptrs that point
        for spPerson01: %d\n\n", numberOfReferencesSecond
        );

}
_cwprintf_s( L"Number of shared_ptrs that point for the
spPerson01: %d\n\n", --numberOfReferencesSecond );

/* Minus one reference to spPerson.  */

spPerson = nullptr;
--numberOfReferencesFirst;

_cwprintf_s( L"Number of shared_ptrs that point for the
spPerson: %d\n\n", numberOfReferencesFirst );
```

```
        Pause();
        _flushall();
        _wsystem( L"cls" );

        return;
};

#pragma endregion

#pragma region Scenario06 - Working with std:move function.

void Scenario06() {

        /*

        RECOMMENDATION

        Except when necessary, do not create multiple owners for
        the same resource.
        This practice add complexity to the source code, and
        application as whole.

        */

        unique_ptr<Person> upPerson { make_unique<Person>()
        }; //Owner
        unique_ptr<Person> upPerson00 { std::move( upPerson ) };
        //  Moving the owner.

        /*

        upPerson not owner anymore.

        */

        /*

        READ ACCESS VIOLATION.
```

The instance of Person object (a resource) was moved
to a new owner, in our example, this new owner is
upPerson00.
After transference, the old reference was reset,
creating null values for internal pointers and random
values for other kinds of data types, such as number
data types.

Our C++ class Person derives of a base class CObject,
one of classes of Microsoft Foundation Classes (MFC)
framework .
One of the methods is CObject->IsSerializable.
After being moved, trying to use the old resource we
have the read access violation because the internal
instance of Person object does not exist anymore.

```
*/
//upPerson->IsSerializable();

Pause();
_flushall();
_wsystem( L"cls" );

return;
};

#pragma endregion

#pragma region  Scenario 07 - Working with weak_ptr and shared_
ptr.

/*
```

A weak_ptr applied for avoid cyclic scenario, A point to B, and
B point to A.

*/

```
void Scenario07() {

        Person* pA { new Person() };
        Person* pB { new Person() };

        shared_ptr<Person> spPersonA { pA }; //Owner
        shared_ptr<Person> spPersonB { pB }; // Owner

        /* Cyclic pointers scenario. */
        //pA->another = pB;
        //pB->another = pA;

        _cwprintf_s( L"Counting for spPersonA BEFORE: %d\
        nCounting for spPersonB BEFORE: %d \n", spPersonA.use_
        count(), spPersonB.use_count() );

        //       delete pB, pB = nullptr, delete pA,
        pA = nullptr;

        _cwprintf_s( L"Counting for spPersonA AFTER: %d\
        nCounting for spPersonB AFTER: %d \n", spPersonA.use_
        count(), spPersonB.use_count() );

        Pause();
        _flushall();
        _wsystem( L"cls" );

        _cwprintf_s( L"Now, using weak_ptr\n \n" );

        _cwprintf_s( L"Counting for spPersonA BEFORE: %d\
        nCounting for spPersonB BEFORE: %d \n", spPersonA.use_
        count(), spPersonB.use_count() );

        weak_ptr<Person> wpPersonA (  spPersonB );  // Take
        ownership temporarily without incrementing the number
        for reference counting.
```

```
weak_ptr<Person> wpPersonB ( spPersonA ); // Take
ownership temporarily without incrementing the number
for reference counting.
```

```
//OR
```

```
//       wpPersonA = spPersonB; // Taking ownership temporarily
without incrementing the number for reference counting.
//       wpPersonB = spPersonA; // Taking ownership temporarily
without incrementing the number for reference counting.
```

```
_cwprintf_s( L"Counting for spPersonA AFTER: %d\
nCounting for spPersonB AFTER: %d \n", spPersonA.use_
count(), spPersonB.use_count() );
```

```
if ( ( !wpPersonA.expired() ) && ( !wpPersonB.expired()
) ) {

        spPersonA = wpPersonA.lock();
        spPersonB = wpPersonB.lock();

        _cwprintf_s( L"Counting for wpPersonA AFTER: %d\
        nCounting for wpPersonB AFTER: %d \n", wpPersonA.
        use_count(), wpPersonB.use_count() );

        _cwprintf_s( L"Counting for spPersonA AFTER: %d\
        nCounting for spPersonB AFTER: %d \n", spPersonA.
        use_count(), spPersonB.use_count() );

        wpPersonA.reset(), wpPersonB.reset();

        _cwprintf_s( L"Counting for wpPersonA AFTER
        reset: %d\nCounting for wpPersonB AFTER reset:
        %d \n", wpPersonA.use_count(), wpPersonB.use_
        count() );
```

```
                _cwprintf_s( L"Counting for spPersonA AFTER
                reset of wpPersonA: %d\nCounting for spPersonB
                AFTER reset of wpPersonB: %d \n", spPersonA.use_
                count(), spPersonB.use_count() );
        };

        return;
};

#pragma endregion

void wmain() {

        Scenario00();

        Scenario01();

        Scenario02();

        Scenario03(); // Learning about Owner

        Scenario04(); // Learning about reference counting

        Scenario05(); // Learning about reference counting using
        scope.

        Scenario06();

        Scenario07();

        Pause( true );

        return;
};
```

The following sections explain each of the functions in the scenarios and give examples.

Scenario00: Show Raw Pointers on an Operation of Assignment with Multiple Pointers

Listing 4-3 demonstrates how to use raw pointers. The purpose is to show that we are responsible for managing the lifetime of the objects pointed at by the raw pointers.

Listing 4-3. Any Number of Pointers Can Point to the Same Instance Through Another Pointer

```
#pragma region Header Files

#include <cstdlib>
#include <cstdint>
#include <cstdio>
#include <memory>
#include <typeinfo>
#include <cwchar>

#include <conio.h>

/* MFC */
#include <afx.h>

/* RVJ */
#include <Utils.h>

#pragma endregion

#pragma region Namespaces

using namespace std;

#pragma endregion

#pragma region Class Person
```

```cpp
class Person : public CObject {

public:
        Person() {

                _cwprintf_s( L"Constructor of Person.\n\n" );

        };
        ~Person() {

                _cwprintf_s( L"Destructor of Person.\n\n" );

        };

public:

        /* Potential for cyclic pointers!!! This is not
        recommended. */
        Person* another {};

};


#pragma endregion

#pragma region Scenario 00 - RAW Pointers

void Scenario00() {

        Person* rPerson { new Person() };
        Person* rPerson00 { rPerson };
        Person* rPerson01 { rPerson };
        Person* rPerson02 { rPerson };

        uint8_t* rUINT8 { new uint8_t( 0x0000 ) };
        uint8_t* rUINT8_00 { rUINT8 };

        uint16_t* rUINT16 { new uint16_t( 0xA000 ) };
        uint16_t* rUINT16_00 { rUINT16 };
```

```cpp
uint32_t* rUINT32 { new uint32_t( 0xC000 ) };
uint32_t* rUINT32_00 { rUINT32 };

uint64_t* rUINT64 { new uint64_t( 0xF000 ) };
uint64_t* rUINT64_00 { rUINT64 };

delete rUINT64_00;
delete rUINT32_00;
delete rUINT16_00;
delete rUINT8_00;
delete rPerson00;

rUINT64     = nullptr;
rUINT64_00 = nullptr;
rUINT32     = nullptr;
rUINT32_00 = nullptr;
rUINT16     = nullptr;
rUINT16_00 = nullptr;
rUINT8      = nullptr;
rUINT8_00  = nullptr;
rPerson     = nullptr;
rPerson00  = nullptr;
rPerson01  = nullptr;
rPerson02  = nullptr;

Pause();
_flushall();
_wsystem( L"cls" );

return;
};
```

```
#pragma endregion

void wmain() {

        Scenario00();
        Pause();

        Pause( true );

        return;
};
```

The figures in this section show the sequence of pointers created to make the points illustrated by the scenario, where two instances of each pointer are pointing to the same instance of a respective target object (in the abstract sense). For example, the rUINT8 and rUINT8_00 instances are pointing to the same instance.

Specifically, Figure 4-2 shows a sequence of code with various raw pointers, more specifically, four raw pointers.

A new instance of the C++ Person class is assigned to the rPerson pointer variable.

The pointer variable rPerson is assigned to the rPerson00, rPerson01, and rPerson02 pointer variables.

This means that all pointer variables (rPerson, rPerson00, rPerson01, and rPerson02) are pointing to the same instance of the C++ class Person.

We can see in the Locals window that all four pointer variables have the same memory address as the assigned value.

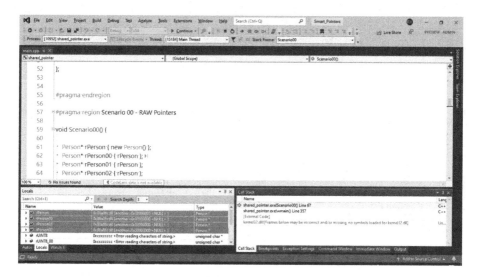

Figure 4-2. *The pointers rPerson, rPerson00, rPerson01, and rPerson02 are pointing to the same instance of an object (an OOP term) of type Person*

Figure 4-3 shows two pointer variables defined, rUINT8 and rUINT8_00.

A new instance of the uint8_t safe integer fundamental type, initialized with a zero value, is assigned to rUINT8.

The pointer variable rUINT8 is assigned to rUINT8_00.

This means that the same memory address that was assigned to rUINT8 was assigned to rUINT8_00.

As a result, both pointer variables rUINT8 and rUINT8_00 are pointing to the same object (an abstract term) instance of the uint8_t type.

We can see in the Locals window that both pointer variables have the same memory address as the assigned value.

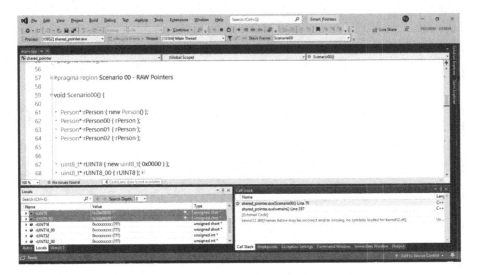

Figure 4-3. *The pointers rUINT8 and rUINT8_00 are pointing to the same instance of an object (an abstract term)*

Figure 4-4 shows two pointer variables defined, rUINT16 and rUINT16_00.

A new instance of the uint16_t safe integer fundamental type, initialized with a nonzero value, is assigned to rUINT16.

The pointer variable rUINT16 is assigned to rUINT16_00.

This means that the same memory address that was assigned to rUINT16 was assigned to rUINT16_00.

As the result, both pointer variables rUINT16 and rUINT16_00 are pointing to the same object (an abstract term) instance of the uint16_t type.

We can see in the Locals window that both pointer variables have the same memory address as the assigned value.

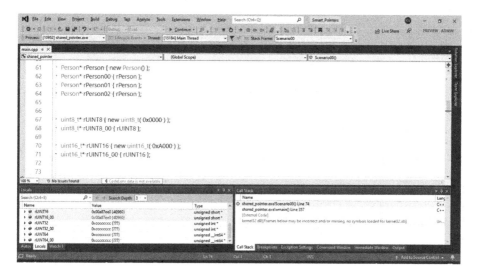

Figure 4-4. *The pointers rUINT16 and rUINT16_00 are pointing to the same instance of an object (an abstract term)*

Figure 4-5 shows two pointer variables defined, rUINT32 and rUINT32_00.

A new instance of the uint32_t safe integer fundamental type, initialized with a nonzero value, is assigned to rUINT32.

The pointer variable rUINT32 is assigned to rUINT32_00.

This means that the same memory address that was assigned to rUINT32 was assigned to rUINT32_00.

As the result, both pointer variables rUINT32 and rUINT32_00 are pointing to the same object (an abstract term) instance of the uint32_t type.

We can see in the Locals window that both pointer variables have the same memory address as the assigned value.

Figure 4-5. *The pointers rUINT32 and rUINT32_00 are pointing to the same instance of an object (an abstract term)*

Figure 4-6 shows two pointer variables defined, rUINT64 and rUINT64_00.

A new instance of the uint64_t safe integer fundamental type, initialized with a nonzero value, is assigned to rUINT64.

The pointer variable rUINT64 is assigned to rUINT64_00.

This means that rUINT64_00 was assigned the same memory address that was assigned to rUINT64.

As the result, both pointer variables rUINT64 and rUINT64_00 are pointing to the same object (an abstract term) instance of the uint64_t type.

We can see in the Locals window that both pointer variables have the same memory address as the assigned value.

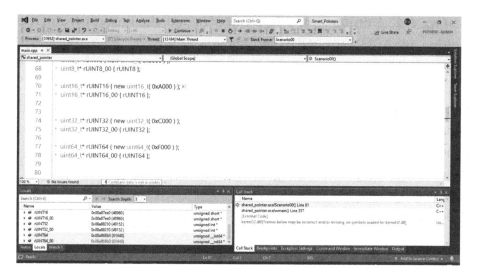

Figure 4-6. *The pointers rUINT64 and rUINT64_00 are pointing to the same instance of an object (an abstract term)*

Scenario01: Out of Scope Is Destroyed

Listing 4-4 shows an example of a `unique_ptr` smart pointer.

Here we open two scopes, one for the function and the other inside the function where the `unique_ptr` smart pointer is created using the `make_unique` template-based function.

The `unique_ptr` smart pointer itself is not created using the global `::new` operator and not removed from memory using the global `::delete` operator.

We are using the `make_unique` template-based function that internally uses the global `::new` operator to create the resource that it owns, in this case an instance of a `Person` object (an OOP term).

Right before it is out of the scope, the global `::delete` operator destroys the owned resource. After that, the `unique_ptr` smart pointer is automatically destroyed from memory.

Listing 4-4. A unique_ptr When Out of Scope, the Resource, and the unique_ptr Are Destroyed in Sequence

```
#pragma region Header Files

#include <cstdlib>
#include <cstdint>
#include <cstdio>
#include <memory>
#include <typeinfo>
#include <cwchar>

#include <conio.h>

/* MFC */
#include <afx.h>

/* RVJ */
#include <Utils.h>

#pragma endregion

#pragma region Namespaces

using namespace std;

#pragma endregion

#pragma region Class Person

class Person : public CObject {

public:
    Person() {

        _cwprintf_s( L"Constructor of Person.\n\n" );

    };
```

```cpp
        ~Person() {

                _cwprintf_s( L"Destructor of Person.\n\n" );

        };
public:

        /* Potential for cyclic pointers!!! This is not
        recommended. */
        Person* another {};

};

#pragma endregion

#pragma region Scenario01 - unique_ptr Smart Pointer

void Scenario01() {

        {

                unique_ptr<Person> upPerson { make_unique<Person>() };

        };

        // Out of scope is destroyed from memory.

        return;
};

#pragma endregion

void wmain() {

        Scenario01();
        Pause();

        Pause( true );

        return;
};
```

Figure 4-7 shows the sequence of code where a new scope is opened inside the Scenario01() function.

Inside this new block, a new instance of the unique_ptr smart pointer is created using the template-based function named make_unique.

In the Locals window, we can see the upPerson variable of the unique_ptr smart pointer.

When the sequence of execution is outside of the block, the instance of unique_ptr is destroyed automatically.

For this sequence of creation of the instance and of destruction of the instance, we have not used the typical global operators ::new and ::delete or the CRT/UCRT functions such as malloc() and free() for memory allocation and memory release.

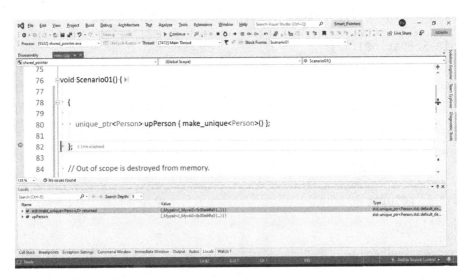

Figure 4-7. *The resources kept by smart pointers when out of scope are destroyed automatically just like any typical object (a generic term)*

Figure 4-8 shows the Locals window but does not show the upPerson unique_ptr smart pointer instance anymore.

This is because the instance of the smart pointer is out of scope at this point and was automatically destroyed.

Figure 4-8.   *The resource and smart pointer not available anymore*

Scenario02: Two Instances of unique_ptr Cannot Point to the Same Instance

As shown in Listing 4-5, there are two instances of unique_ptr, and when using a unique_ptr smart pointer, only one unique_ptr can point to an instance.

Here we have two scopes, one for the function and the other one for the example of unique_ptr. Removing the comment, the code analysis shows an error before the build process begins.

The Error List window shows the details of the errors of a second unique_ptr trying to point to the same instance of a resource kept by the first unique_ptr.

Listing 4-5. Two Instances of unique_ptr Cannot Point to the Same Instance

```
#pragma region Header Files

#include <cstdlib>
#include <cstdint>
#include <cstdio>
#include <memory>
#include <typeinfo>
#include <cwchar>

#include <conio.h>

/* MFC */
#include <afx.h>

/* RVJ */
#include <Utils.h>

#pragma endregion

#pragma region Namespaces

using namespace std;

#pragma endregion

#pragma region Class Person

class Person : public CObject {

public:
      Person() {

            _cwprintf_s( L"Constructor of Person.\n\n" );

      };
```

```cpp
        ~Person() {

                _cwprintf_s( L"Destructor of Person.\n\n" );

        };

public:

        /* Potential for cyclic pointers!!! This is not
        recommended. */
        Person* another {};

};

#pragma endregion

#pragma region Scenario02 - unique_ptr Smart Pointer

/* Two instances of unique_ptr cannot points to the same
instance. */
void Scenario02() {

        {

                unique_ptr<Person> upPerson { make_
                unique<Person>() };
                /* unique_ptr<Person> upPerson00 { upPerson }; */

        };

        // Out of scope, the smart pointer is destroyed from
        memory.

        Pause();
        _flushall();
        _wsystem( L"cls" );

        return;
};
```

```
#pragma endregion
void wmain() {

        Scenario00();

        Scenario01();

        Scenario02();

        Pause( true );

        return;
};
```

Figure 4-9 shows the sequence of code that creates a unique_ptr instance.

We also have a second unique_ptr, which is not available yet, pointing to the same instance.

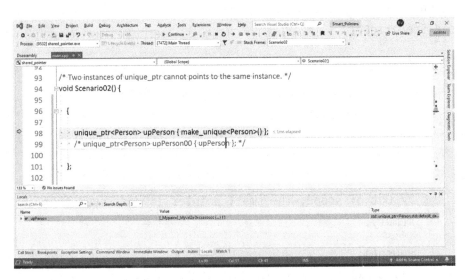

Figure 4-9. *Example of creation of a unique_ptr. The second unique_ptr pointing to the same instance is not available yet*

Figure 4-10 shows the code sequence where we have two scopes, one for the Scenario02() function and the other for the unique_ptr smart pointer variables upPerson and upPerson00.

Two instances of the unique_ptr smart pointer cannot point to the same instance, and by removing the comment, the code analysis shows an error before the build process begins. That is, we cannot write code like this because it results in an error.

The Smart Analysis tip message shows details of the error about a second unique_ptr upPerson00 trying to point to the same instance of a resource kept by the first unique_ptr upPerson.

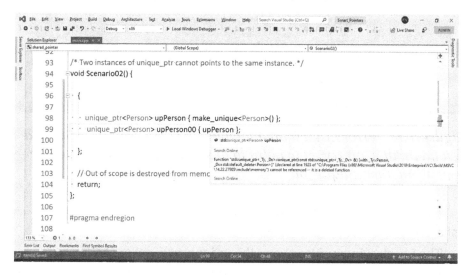

Figure 4-10. *After removing the comment, the code analysis indicates an error before the build process begins*

Figure 4-11 shows the Error List window with details about a second unique_ptr upPerson00 trying to point to the same instance of a resource kept by the first unique_ptr upPerson.

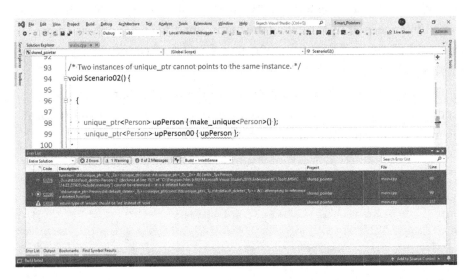

Figure 4-11. *Error List window showing the details of the errors of a second unique_ptr trying to point to the same instance of a resource kept by another unique_ptr*

Figure 4-12 shows two sequence of code where the unique_ptr upPerson is valid when is in an active scope.

The Locals window also shows the unique_ptr upPerson smart pointer variable and the resource kept by the smart pointer.

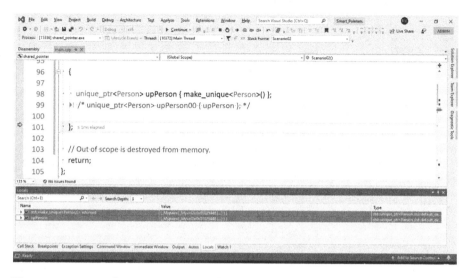

Figure 4-12. *When going out of scope, the resources kept by two smart pointers are not valid anymore*

Figure 4-13 shows the sequence of code at a point of execution where the unique_ptr smart pointer's upPerson variable is not valid anymore; it is out of scope.

Because of this, the unique_ptr smart pointer's upPerson is not shown in the Locals window.

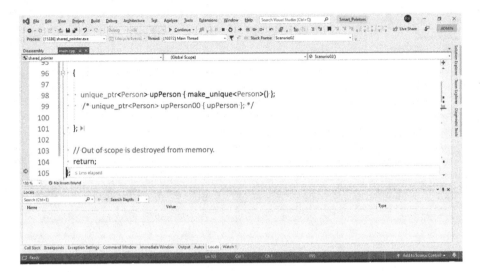

Figure 4-13. *When out of scope, the resources kept by two smart pointers are automatically destroyed*

Scenario03: Owner Concept

As shown in Listing 4-6, there are three owners for three different resources, respectively, and two references for an existing smart pointer and respective resource. The owner counts as one reference.

Anytime we have more than one reference to the same smart pointer, the reference counter is incremented by one.

Anytime we have a reference to the same smart pointer removed, the reference counter is decremented by one.

Listing 4-6. Learning About the Owner Concept

```
#pragma region Header Files

#include <cstdlib>
#include <cstdint>
#include <cstdio>
#include <memory>
```

```cpp
#include <typeinfo>
#include <cwchar>

#include <conio.h>

/* MFC */
#include <afx.h>

/* RVJ */
#include <Utils.h>

#pragma endregion

#pragma region Namespaces

using namespace std;

#pragma endregion

#pragma region Class Person

class Person : public CObject {

public:
        Person() {

                _cwprintf_s( L"Constructor of Person.\n\n" );

        };
        ~Person() {

                _cwprintf_s( L"Destructor of Person.\n\n" );

        };
```

```
public:

        /* Potential for cyclic pointers!!! This is not
        recommended. */
        Person* another {};

};

#pragma endregion

#pragma region Scenario03 - shared_ptr Smart Pointer - Learning
about owner concept.

void Scenario03() {

        shared_ptr<Person> spPerson { make_shared<Person>() };
        // Owner
        shared_ptr<Person> spPerson00 { spPerson }; // Not
        owner, just a new reference.
        shared_ptr<Person> spPerson01 { make_shared<Person>() };
        // Owner
        shared_ptr<Person> spPerson02 { new Person() }; // Owner

        _cwprintf_s( L"Number of shared_ptr that points to the
        same resource: %d\n\n", spPerson.use_count() );

        if ( const wchar_t* yes_or_no = YesOrNo( spPerson01.
        owner_before( spPerson ) ) ) {

                _cwprintf_s( L"Owner before on hierarchy:
                %s\n\n", yes_or_no );

        };

        Pause();
        _flushall();
```

```
    _wsystem( L"cls" );

    return;
};
```

```
#pragma endregion
```

Figure 4-14 shows the sequence of source code for the concept of ownership when working with the shared_ptr smart pointer.

We have two owners, spPerson and spPerson01, defined through the template-based function make_shared.

We also have one reference provided by the spPerson00 shared_ptr smart pointer to the first owner that is the spPerson shared_ptr smart pointer.

When the smart pointer is created by using the make_shared template function, we have an owner.

When the smart pointer is created by using the global operator ::new, we also have the definition of an owner.

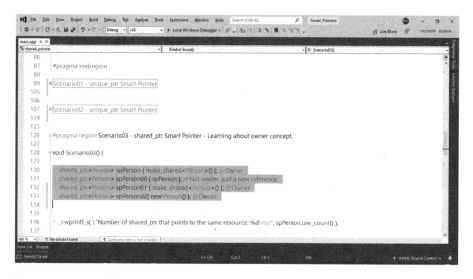

Figure 4-14. *The sequence for the concept of ownership*

Figure 4-15 shows the sequence of the source code during execution where we have three owners: spPerson, spPerson01, and spPerson02.

The two owners spPerson and spPerson01 were created using the templated-based function make_shared, which creates an instance of a smart pointer of type shared_ptr.

The owner spPerson02 is a shared_ptr smart pointer, but the resource kept by the smart pointer was created using the global operator ::new.

We also have two references to the same instance, spPerson and spPerson00. This is because the owner also counts as a reference.

Because of this, the result for calling the spPerson.use_count() member function is 2, which means that we have two instances of the shared_ptr smart pointers pointing to the same instance of a resource, in this case, an instance of C++ class Person.

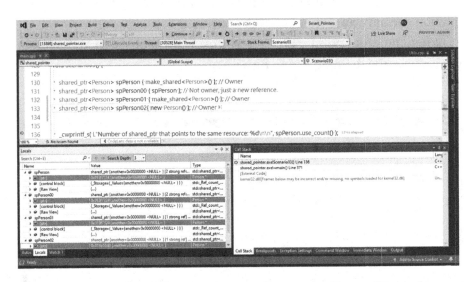

Figure 4-15. *We have three owners, spPerson, spPerson01, and spPerson02, and two references to the same instance, spPerson and spPerson00*

Figure 4-16 shows a sequence of source code where we have one owner and two references.

The owner is the shared_ptr smart pointer called spPerson that also is a reference.

The shared_ptr smart pointer spPerson00 is a reference for the same smart pointer and respective resource.

Figure 4-16. *Here we have one owner and two references, spPerson and spPerson00, for the same smart pointer and respective resource*

Figure 4-17 shows the results for the reference counting of spPerson.

In this case we have the value 2 because the owner spPerson also counts as a reference.

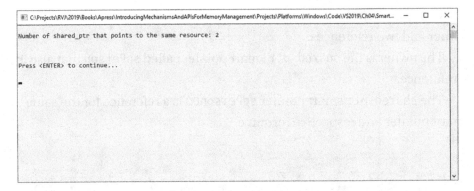

Figure 4-17. *The results for the reference counting of spPerson*

Scenario04: Overview of Reference Counting Using Scope

As shown in Listing 4-7, in this scenario we are working with reference counting using one level for the scope; two owners, spPerson and spPerson01; and two references to the same resource, spPerson and spPerson00.

Listing 4-7. Reference Counting Using Scope

```
#pragma region Header Files

#include <cstdlib>
#include <cstdint>
#include <cstdio>
#include <memory>
#include <typeinfo>
#include <cwchar>

#include <conio.h>

/* MFC */
#include <afx.h>
```

```cpp
/* RVJ */
#include <Utils.h>

#pragma endregion

#pragma region Namespaces

using namespace std;

#pragma endregion

#pragma region Class Person

class Person : public CObject {
public:
        Person() {

                _cwprintf_s( L"Constructor of Person.\n\n" );

        };
        ~Person() {

                _cwprintf_s( L"Destructor of Person.\n\n" );

        };
public:

        /* Potential for cyclic pointers!!! This is not
        recommended. */
        Person* another {};

};

#pragma endregion
```

```
#pragma region Scenario04 - shared_ptr Smart Pointer - Learning
about reference counting concept.

void Scenario04() {

        shared_ptr<Person> spPerson { make_shared<Person>() };
        // Owner
        shared_ptr<Person> spPerson01 { make_shared<Person>() };
        // Owner

        long numberOfReferencesFirst { spPerson.use_count() };
        long numberOfReferencesSecond { spPerson01.use_count() };

        _cwprintf_s( L"Number of shared_ptrs that point for the
        spPerson: %d\n\n", numberOfReferencesFirst );

        shared_ptr<Person> spPerson00 { spPerson }; // Not
        owner, just a new reference.

        numberOfReferencesFirst = spPerson00.use_count();

        _cwprintf_s( L"Number of shared_ptrs that point for the
        spPerson: %d\n\n", numberOfReferencesFirst );

        _cwprintf_s( L"Number of shared_ptrs that point for the
        spPerson01: %d\n\n", numberOfReferencesSecond );

        /* Minus one reference to spPerson.  */
        spPerson00 = nullptr;
        --numberOfReferencesFirst;

        _cwprintf_s( L"Number of shared_ptrs that point for the
        spPerson: %d\n\n", numberOfReferencesFirst );

        /* Minus one reference to spPerson.  */
        spPerson = nullptr;
        --numberOfReferencesFirst;
```

```
_cwprintf_s( L"Number of shared_ptrs that point for the
spPerson: %d\n\n", numberOfReferencesFirst );

_cwprintf_s( L"Number of shared_ptrs that point for the
spPerson01: %d\n\n", numberOfReferencesSecond );

spPerson01 = nullptr;
--numberOfReferencesSecond;

_cwprintf_s( L"Number of shared_ptrs that point for the
spPerson01: %d\n\n", numberOfReferencesSecond );

Pause();
_flushall();
_wsystem( L"cls" );

return;
};
```

#pragma endregion

Figure 4-18 shows a sequence of code with two owners and two references.

The owners are the shared_ptr smart pointers spPerson and spPerson01, both defined using the template-based function make_shared.

We also have two references to the same resource, the shared_ptr smart pointers spPerson and spPerson00.

We must be aware that every owner is also a reference, so it counts the number of references pointing to the resource.

Highlighted in the Locals window we have three shared_ptr smart pointers named spPerson, spPerson00, and spPerson01 showing this scenario for reference counting.

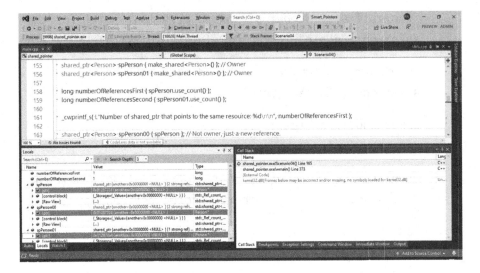

Figure 4-18. *Here we have two owners, spPerson and spPerson01, and two references to the same resource, spPerson and spPerson00*

Figure 4-19 shows the results of reference counting implemented by the sample source code.

The first result, the value 1, indicates that spPerson, which is the owner, is also the only reference to the resource assigned to it.

The second result, the value 2, indicates that spPerson has another reference to the resource that it owns.

The second reference in this case is the shared_ptr smart pointer spPerson00.

The third result, the value 1, is about the other owner, the shared_ptr smart pointer spPerson01.

We must remember that every owner is also a reference.

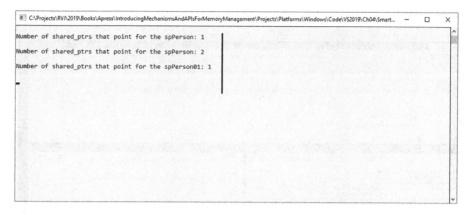

Figure 4-19. *Showing the results of reference counting*

Figure 4-20 shows the sequence of code where we have a decrement in the number of references to a resource.

The shared_ptr smart pointer spPerson00 is not an owner; it is only a reference to the same resource owned by the shared_ptr smart pointer spPerson, which is an owner of a resource.

Assigning nullptr to the shared_ptr smart pointer spPerson00 that is a reference, we have one less reference to the same resource owned by the shared_ptr smart pointer spPerson.

This happens because the shared_ptr smart pointer spPerson00 is not a reference anymore.

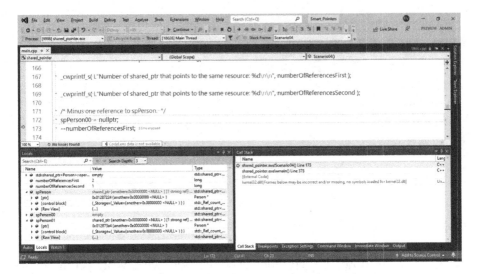

Figure 4-20. *Assigning nullptr to reference spPerson00, we have one less reference to the same instance, spPerson, because spPerson00 is not a reference anymore*

Figure 4-21 shows the same first three results of reference counting implemented by the sample source code shown in Figure 4-19, but with a fourth result.

This fourth result, the value 1, is about the decrement of references, because we assigned `nullptr` to the `shared_ptr` smart pointer `spPerson00`, which was a reference to the resource owned by the `shared_ptr` smart pointer `spPerson`.

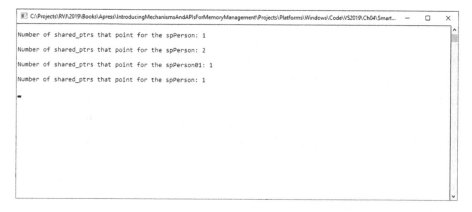

Figure 4-21. *Showing the results of reference counting*

Figure 4-22 shows a sequence of code where the owner is destroyed.

In this sequence, the owner `shared_ptr` smart pointer `spPerson` is assigned the `nullptr` value.

After this, the result of reference counting is zero for the first smart pointer `spPerson`.

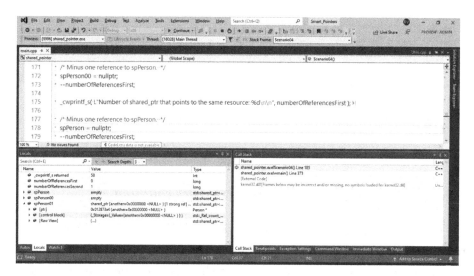

Figure 4-22. *Here we have the spPerson resource and smart pointer being destroyed. After this, the result of counting is zero for the first smart pointer spPerson*

Figure 4-23 shows the same results of reference counting implemented by the sample source code and shown in Figure 4-19 and Figure 4-21, but with two new messages.

As we have assigned the `nullptr` value to the `shared_ptr` smart pointer `spPerson`, the resource of type C++ class `Person`, has a destructor called, because the instance will also be destroyed automatically by the smart pointer's internal implementation.

Because of this assignment of the `nullptr` value for the `shared_ptr` smart pointer `spPerson`, a fifth result, the value 0, specifies the number of references of the smart pointer `spPerson`.

The sixth result, the value 1, is about the other owner, the `shared_ptr` smart pointer `spPerson01`.

The `shared_ptr` smart pointer `spPerson01` has only itself as a reference; because of this, it has 1 for the reference count value.

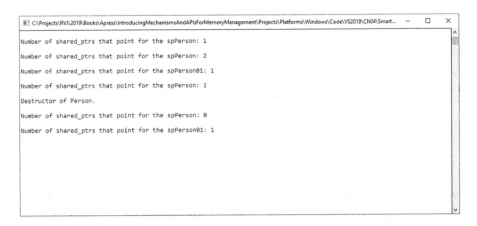

Figure 4-23. Showing the results of reference counting

Figure 4-24 shows the sequence of code that destroys an owner of a resource.

In this sequence of code, we have the `shared_ptr` smart pointer `spPerson01` and the resource owned by the smart pointer being destroyed.

After this sequence of destruction, the result of counting is zero for the second smart pointer spPerson01.

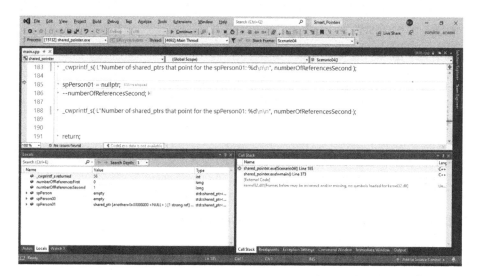

Figure 4-24. *Here we have the spPerson01 resource and smart pointer being destroyed. After this, the result of counting is zero for the second smart pointer spPerson01*

Figure 4-25 shows the same results of reference counting implemented by the sample source code and shown in Figure 4-19, Figure 4-21, and Figure 4-23, but with two new messages for results.

As we have assigned the nullptr value to the shared_ptr smart pointer spPerson01, the resource of type C++ class Person has a destructor called because the instance will also be destroyed automatically by the smart pointer's internal implementation.

Because of this assignment of the nullptr value to the shared_ptr smart pointer spPerson01, a seventh result, the value 0, is about the number of references to the smart pointer spPerson01.

```
C:\Projects\RV\2019\Books\Apress\IntroducingMechanismsAndAPIsForMemoryManagement\Projects\Platforms\Windows\Code\VS2019\Ch04\Smart...   —   □   ×

Number of shared_ptrs that point for the spPerson: 1

Number of shared_ptrs that point for the spPerson: 2

Number of shared_ptrs that point for the spPerson01: 1

Number of shared_ptrs that point for the spPerson: 1

Destructor of Person.

Number of shared_ptrs that point for the spPerson: 0

Number of shared_ptrs that point for the spPerson01: 1

Destructor of Person.

Number of shared_ptrs that point for the spPerson01: 0
```

Figure 4-25. *The results of reference counting*

Scenario05: More Details About Reference Counting Using Scope

Listing 4-8 presents a scenario similar to the previous scenario, but the code uses two scopes instead of one. We also show more figures to illustrate the steps.

Listing 4-8. Reference Counting Using Scope

```
#pragma region Header Files

#include <cstdlib>
#include <cstdint>
#include <cstdio>
#include <memory>
#include <typeinfo>
#include <cwchar>
```

```cpp
#include <conio.h>

/* MFC */
#include <afx.h>

/* RVJ */
#include <Utils.h>

#pragma endregion

#pragma region Namespaces

using namespace std;

#pragma endregion

#pragma region Class Person

class Person : public CObject {

public:

        Person() {

                _cwprintf_s( L"Constructor of Person.\n\n" );

        };
        ~Person() {

                _cwprintf_s( L"Destructor of Person.\n\n" );

        };

public:

        /* Potential for cyclic pointers!!! This is not
        recommended. */
        Person* another {};

};
```

```
#pragma endregion

#pragma region Scenario05 - shared_ptr Smart Pointer - Learning
about reference counting using scope.

void Scenario05() {

        shared_ptr<Person> spPerson { make_shared<Person>() };
        // Owner

        long numberOfReferencesFirst { spPerson.use_count() };
        long numberOfReferencesSecond {};

        _cwprintf_s( L"Number of shared_ptrs that point for the
        spPerson: %d\n\n", numberOfReferencesFirst );

        {

                /* Open scope. More one reference for spPerson. */
                shared_ptr<Person> spPerson00 { spPerson };
                // Not owner, just a new reference.

                numberOfReferencesFirst = spPerson.use_count();

                _cwprintf_s( L"Number of shared_ptrs that point
                for spPerson: %d\n\n", numberOfReferencesFirst );

        }

        /* Closed scope. Minus  one reference for spPerson. */
        numberOfReferencesFirst = spPerson.use_count();

        _cwprintf_s( L"Number of shared_ptrs that point for
        spPerson: %d\n\n", numberOfReferencesFirst );

        {
```

```
            shared_ptr<Person> spPerson01 { make_
            shared<Person>() }; // Owner

            numberOfReferencesSecond = spPerson01.use_
            count();

            _cwprintf_s( L"Number of shared_ptrs that point for
            spPerson01: %d\n\n", numberOfReferencesSecond );

    }
    _cwprintf_s( L"Number of shared_ptrs that point for the
    spPerson01: %d\n\n", --numberOfReferencesSecond );

    /* Minus one reference to spPerson.  */

    spPerson = nullptr;
    --numberOfReferencesFirst;

    _cwprintf_s( L"Number of shared_ptrs that point for the
    spPerson: %d\n\n", numberOfReferencesFirst );

    Pause();
    _flushall();
    _wsystem( L"cls" );

    return;
};

#pragma endregion
```

Figure 4-26 shows the sequence of code with a smart pointer and a resource with a function scope. We have defined the shared_ptr smart pointer spPerson using the template-based function make_shared. After creation, we have an owner and a reference to the resource through the smart pointer. At this point in execution, the reference counting number for the shared_ptr smart pointer spPerson owned resource is 1.

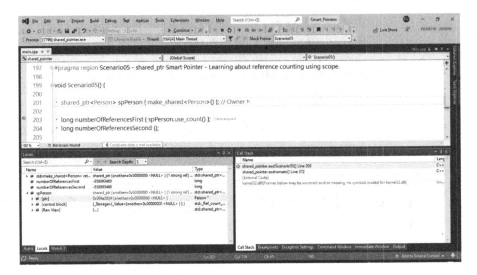

Figure 4-26. *First smart pointer and resource with function scope*

Figure 4-27 shows two sequence of code where a new scope is opened inside the Scenario05() function and where a new reference is created for an existing smart pointer resource.

The shared_ptr smart pointer spPerson00 is not a new owner, just a new reference for spPerson and the owned resource.

The difference is that the shared_ptr smart pointer spPerson00 is in another scope, not in the function scope.

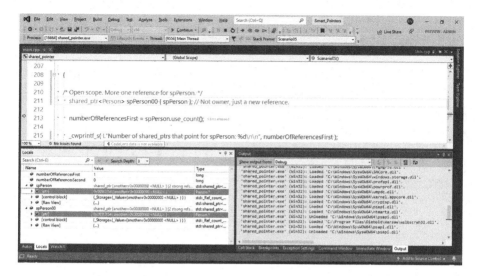

Figure 4-27. *Not a new owner, just a new reference for spPerson and the resource*

Figure 4-28 shows the sequence of code where the number of references to spPerson appears.

At this point in the execution, the number of items pointing to the spPerson is 1.

We must remember that the owner is automatically a reference to the resource that it owns. So, every owner count is increased by one for the number of references to the resource owned by itself.

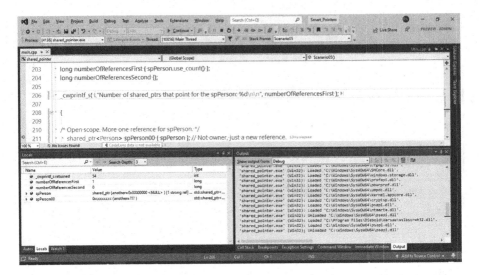

Figure 4-28. *Showing the number of items pointing to spPerson to manage the lifetime of a resource*

Figure 4-29 shows the number of references to the shared_ptr smart pointer spPerson and the owned resource.

At this point in execution, the number of references is increased by one.

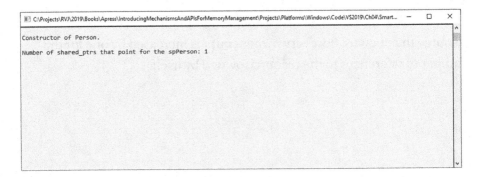

Figure 4-29. *Showing the results of reference counting*

Figure 4-30 shows the sequence of code where a new reference is created to the existing spPerson smart pointer and the owned resource.

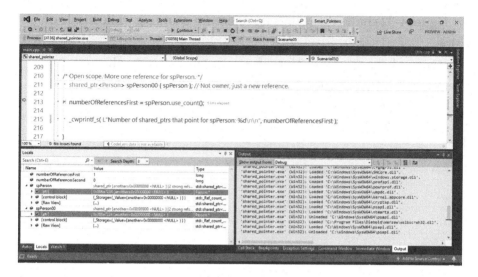

Figure 4-30. *Open new block (new scope), create a new reference for spPerson, and increase the number for references*

Figure 4-31 shows the results for reference counting while inside scope.

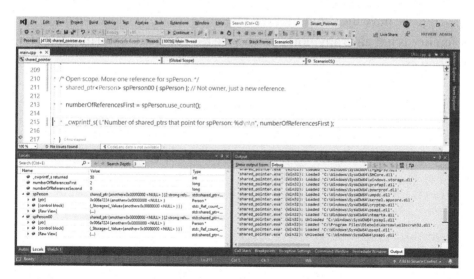

Figure 4-31. *Showing the results of reference counting while inside of scope*

121

Figure 4-32 shows the results for reference counting while inside of scope.

Here we have the value 2 for reference count, because the new reference is still alive inside the new scope.

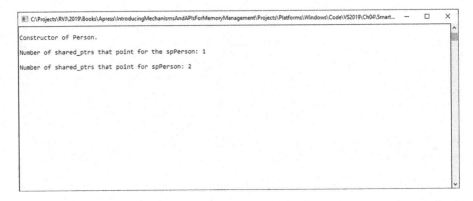

Figure 4-32. *Showing the results of reference counting while in scope*

Figure 4-33 shows the results of reference counting when outside of scope.

Here we have the value 1 for the reference count, because the new reference is not alive anymore, so we have a decrement in the number of references.

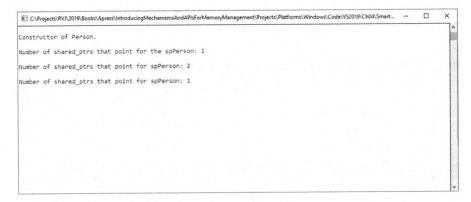

Figure 4-33. *Showing the results of reference counting when out of scope*

Figure 4-34 shows a number of references for spPerson01 while in scope.

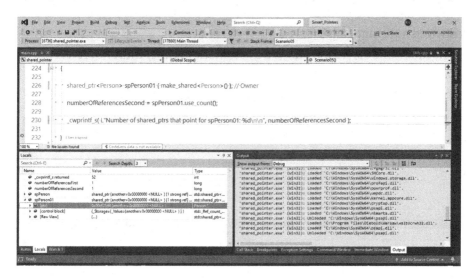

Figure 4-34. *Showing the results of reference counting for spPerson01 while in scope*

Figure 4-35 shows a number of references for spPerson01 that in this sequence of code is 1.

We must remember that the owner counts as one reference, and because of this, for spPerson01 that is an owner, we also have a reference.

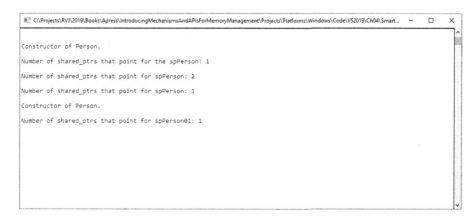

Figure 4-35. *Showing the results of reference counting for spPerson01*

Figure 4-36 shows that the spPerson01 smart pointer is destroyed.

This happens because we are out of scope, and the smart pointer is destroyed automatically.

Because of this, we also have a decrement in the number of references.

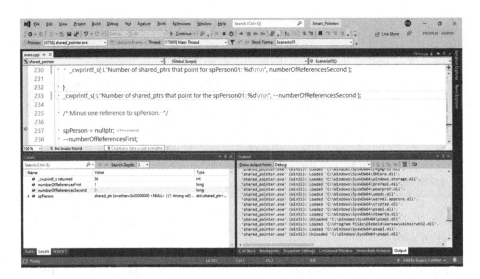

Figure 4-36. *Showing the results of reference counting for spPerson01 when out of scope*

Figure 4-37 shows a sequence of code where the nullptr value is assigned to the smart pointer.

Assigning nullptr to spPerson, the resource owned is destroyed, but the smart pointer is still alive and ready to take new ownership via a new assignment while in scope.

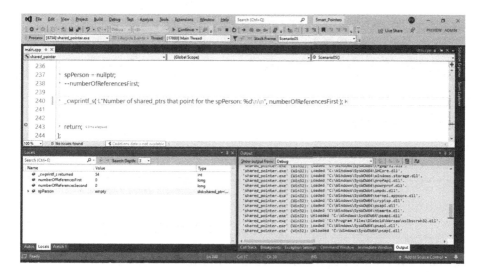

Figure 4-37. *Assigning nullptr to spPerson. The resource is destroyed, but the smart pointer is still alive and ready to take new ownership via a new assignment while in scope*

Figure 4-38 shows a sequence with the result of reference counting after all the references have been destroyed.

Of course, the result of the number of references for spPerson and spPerson01 is 0 because all references are destroyed for any of these smart pointers and for the owned resources of each one.

```
C:\Projects\RVJ\2019\Books\Apress\IntroducingMechanismsAndAPIsForMemoryManagement\Projects\Platforms\Windows\Code\VS2019\Ch04\Smart...   —   □   ×

Constructor of Person.

Number of shared_ptrs that point for the spPerson: 1

Number of shared_ptrs that point for spPerson: 2

Number of shared_ptrs that point for spPerson: 1

Constructor of Person.

Number of shared_ptrs that point for spPerson01: 1

Destructor of Person.

Number of shared_ptrs that point for the spPerson01: 0

Destructor of Person.

Number of shared_ptrs that point for the spPerson: 0
```

Figure 4-38. *Showing the final results of the reference counting for all shared_ptrs smart pointers*

Scenario 06: Working with the std::move Template Function

This scenario shows how to work with the std::move template function.

Characteristics of unique_ptr, shared_ptr, and Owner Concept

The unique_ptr smart pointer cannot be shared or copied, only moved. This section highlights some notable characteristics of unique_ptr.

As shown in Listing 4-9, the same instance of unique_ptr cannot be assigned to another variable of type unique_ptr.

The smart pointer unique_ptr template class implementation has overridden the assignment operator, which avoids the concept of being shared or copied.

Being moved means that a new instance of unique_ptr is created and becomes the owner of the resource instance kept by the source instance of unique_ptr.

Moving between smart pointers of type unique_ptr does *not* mean copying the state from the source instance for the new instance, as in OOP.

Copying in the traditional OOP sense means having one or more copy constructors that do the copying of state of the source object instance to the target object instance.

When using the function std::move, we get a new instance that becomes the owner of the source object instance; however, destroying the instance of the resource object as a tacit rule is not optional.

Listing 4-9. The Only Way to Transfer the Ownership for an Instance of unique_ptr Is to Use the std::move Function

```
#pragma region Header Files

#include <cstdlib>
#include <cstdint>
#include <cstdio>
#include <memory>
#include <typeinfo>
#include <cwchar>

#include <conio.h>

/* MFC */
#include <afx.h>

/* RVJ */
#include <Utils.h>

#pragma endregion

#pragma region Namespaces

using namespace std;

#pragma endregion
```

```cpp
#pragma region Class Person

class Person : public CObject {

public:

        Person() {

                _cwprintf_s( L"Constructor of Person.\n\n" );

        };
        ~Person() {

                _cwprintf_s( L"Destructor of Person.\n\n" );

        };

public:

        /* Potential for cyclic pointers!!! This is not
        recommended. */
        Person* another {};

};

#pragma endregion

#pragma region Scenario06 - Working with std:move function.

void Scenario06() {

        unique_ptr<Person> upPerson { make_unique<Person>() };
        //Owner
        unique_ptr<Person> upPerson00 { std::move( upPerson ) };
        //  Moving the owner.

        /*

        upPerson not owner anymore.

        */
```

```
        upPerson->IsSerializable();

        Pause();
        _flushall();
        _wsystem( L"cls" );

        return;
};

#pragma endregion
```

Recommendation   Except when absolutely necessary, do not create multiple owners for the same resource. This practice adds complexity to the source code and to the software application as a whole.

Read Access Violation

The instance of a Person object (a resource) was moved to a new owner in our example, with the new owner being upPerson00.

After the transfer, the old reference was reset, creating null values for internal pointers and random values for other kinds of data types, such as numbers.

Our class Person derives from the abstract base class CObject, one of fundamental classes of the Microsoft Foundation Classes (MFC) framework.

One of the methods is CObject->IsSerializable().

After being moved, trying to access the previous resource via an early owner causes a read access violation because the internal pointer for the instance of the Person object does not exist anymore.

Figure 4-39 shows the sequence of code that moves the owner of a resource.

In this sequence, we have used the upPerson00 unique_ptr to be the new owner of the resources previously owned by the unique_ptr upPerson.

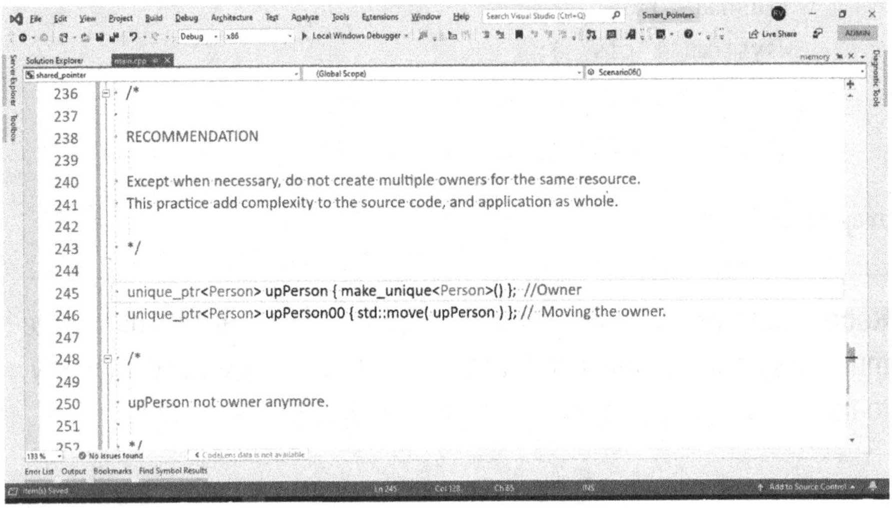

Figure 4-39. *Moving the owner*

Figure 4-40 shows the sequence of code with the state of the smart pointers before the execution of the std::move template-based function.

The Locals window shows the state of both instances before the transfer of the owner from one smart pointer to another smart pointer.

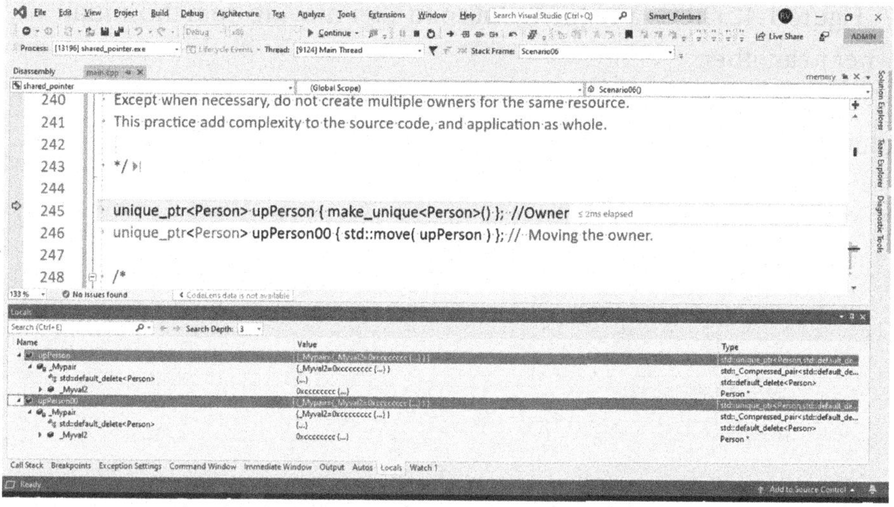

Figure 4-40. *Before moving from one owner to another*

Figure 4-41 shows a sequence of code with the state of smart pointers before the execution of the `std::move` template-based function.

The Locals window shows the state of both instances before the transfer of the owner from one smart pointer to another smart pointer.

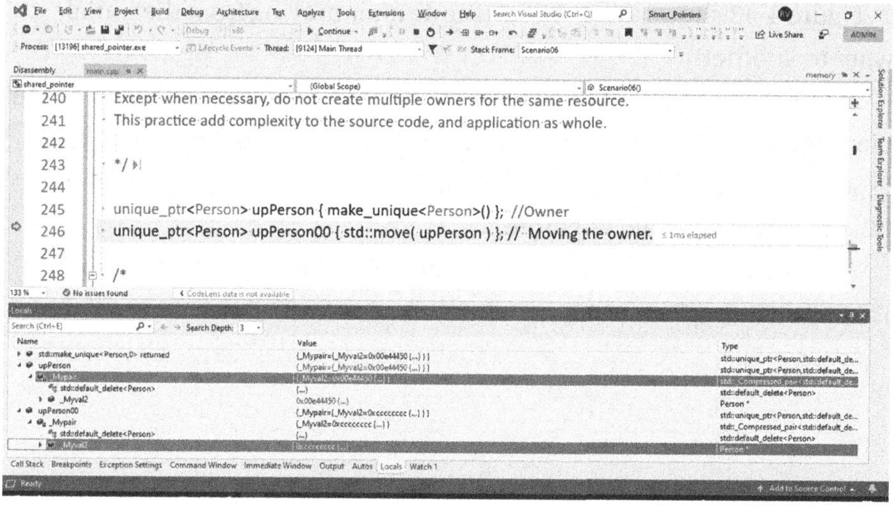

Figure 4-41. *Before execution of the std::move template function*

Figure 4-42 shows a sequence of code after moving from the initial owner to another.

The Locals window shows the state of the instances of the smart pointers and resources just after transferring the owner.

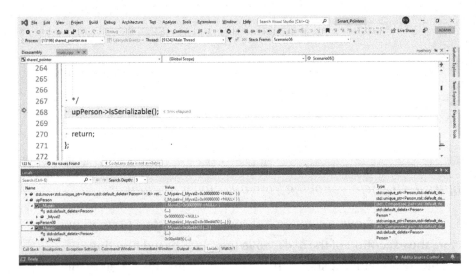

Figure 4-42. *After moving from the initial owner to another*

Figure 4-43 shows a sequence of code after moving from the initial owner to another.

At this point of execution, upPerson is not an owner of the MFC Person object and is trying to call an instance member function named CObject->IsSerializable(). Trying to use a method of the source through the initial owner is not valid anymore.

The instance of the C++ class Person, the owned resource, was moved to a new owner, upPerson00.

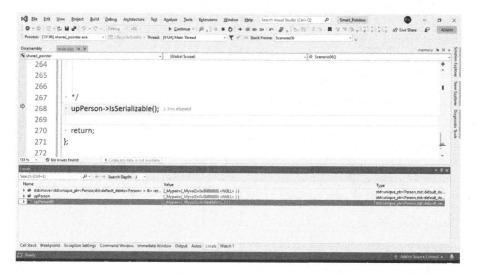

Figure 4-43. *Trying to use a method of the source through the initial owner is not valid anymore*

Figure 4-44 shows the sequence where the code is trying to access an instance member function of the owned resource.

The result is an exception associated with a read access violation because we are trying to access a resource that does not exist anymore.

Our C++ class Person derives from of a base class CObject, which is part of the MFC framework.

One of the instance member functions of the class MFC CObject is CObject->IsSerializable().

After moving Person, trying to use the resource causes the read access violation because the internal instance of the C++ class Person does not exist anymore through upPerson.

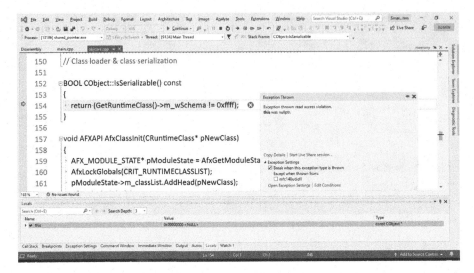

Figure 4-44. *Read access violation trying to access the resource that does not exist anymore*

Scenario 07: Working with the weak_ptr Smart Pointer

The main purpose of an instance of a weak_ptr pointer is to avoid the increment of reference counting when it's necessary that the access to a shared_ptr and the underlying resource is kept by the smart pointer.

So, when you find a weak_ptr pointer, first check the algorithms, the implementation logic of the application, and the scenarios where weak_ptr is in use, and change what is necessary to keep the use of weak_ptr to a minimum.

One possible scenario for using instances of weak_ptr is on a cyclic reference between shared_ptr smart pointer instances, where A points to B, and B points to A.

Listing 4-10 shows how to use weak_ptr.

Listing 4-10. Cyclic Scenario for the Use of weak_ptr

```
#pragma region Header Files

#include <cstdlib>
#include <cstdint>
#include <cstdio>
#include <memory>
#include <typeinfo>
#include <cwchar>

#include <conio.h>

/* MFC */
#include <afx.h>

/* RVJ */
#include <Utils.h>

#pragma endregion

#pragma region Namespaces

using namespace std;

#pragma endregion

#pragma region Class Person

class Person : public CObject {

public:
        Person() {

                _cwprintf_s( L"Constructor of Person.\n\n" );

        };
```

```cpp
    ~Person() {

        _cwprintf_s( L"Destructor of Person.\n\n" );

    };
public:

    /* Potential for cyclic pointers!!! This is not
    recommended. */
    Person* another {};

};

#pragma endregion

#pragma region  Scenario 07 - Working with weak_ptr and shared_
ptr.

/*

A weak_ptr applied for avoid cyclic scenario, A point to B, and
B point to A.

*/

void Scenario07() {

        Person* pA { new Person() };
        Person* pB { new Person() };

        shared_ptr<Person> spPersonA { pA }; //Owner
        shared_ptr<Person> spPersonB { pB }; // Owner

        /* Cyclic pointers scenario. */
        //pA->another = pB;
        //pB->another = pA;
```

```
_cwprintf_s( L"Counting for spPersonA BEFORE: %d\
nCounting for spPersonB BEFORE: %d \n", spPersonA.use_
count(), spPersonB.use_count() );

//    delete pB, pB = nullptr, delete pA, pA = nullptr;

_cwprintf_s( L"Counting for spPersonA AFTER: %d\
nCounting for spPersonB AFTER: %d \n", spPersonA.use_
count(), spPersonB.use_count() );

Pause();
_flushall();
_wsystem( L"cls" );

_cwprintf_s( L"Now, using weak_ptr\n \n" );

_cwprintf_s( L"Counting for spPersonA BEFORE: %d\
nCounting for spPersonB BEFORE: %d \n", spPersonA.use_
count(), spPersonB.use_count() );

weak_ptr<Person> wpPersonA ( spPersonB );  // Take
ownership temporarily without increment the number for
reference counting.
weak_ptr<Person> wpPersonB ( spPersonA ); // Take
ownership temporarily without increment the number for
reference counting.

//OR
```

```
//    wpPersonA = spPersonB; // Taking ownership temporarily
       without increment the number for reference counting.
//    wpPersonB = spPersonA; // Taking ownership temporarily
       without increment the number for reference counting.
```

```
    _cwprintf_s( L"Counting for spPersonA AFTER: %d\
    nCounting for spPersonB AFTER: %d \n", spPersonA.
    use_count(), spPersonB.use_count() );

    if( ( !wpPersonA.expired() ) && ( !wpPersonB.expired()
    ) ) {

        spPersonA = wpPersonA.lock();
        spPersonB = wpPersonB.lock();

        _cwprintf_s( L"Counting for wpPersonA AFTER: %d\
        nCounting for wpPersonB AFTER: %d \n", wpPersonA.
        use_count(), wpPersonB.use_count() );

        wpPersonA.reset(), wpPersonB.reset();

        _cwprintf_s( L"Counting for wpPersonA AFTER reset:
        %d\nCounting for wpPersonB AFTER reset: %d \n",
        wpPersonA.use_count(), wpPersonB.use_count() );

    };

    return;
};

#pragma endregion
```

Figure 4-45 shows the two owners defined.

We have a sequence where there are two raw pointers that will be used to create and initialize the two shared_ptr smart pointers that own the resources, that is, the two instances of the C++ class Person.

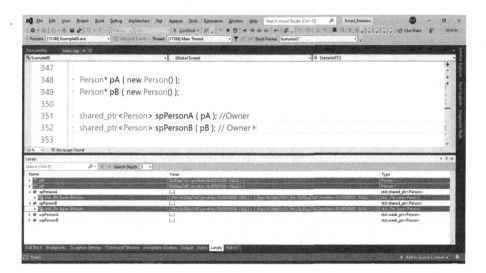

Figure 4-45. *Shared pointer spPersonA is the owner of resource pA, and spPersonB is the owner of pB*

Figure 4-46 shows the results of reference counting for spPersonA and spPersonB without using a weak_ptr.

The first two results, showing 1 and the word BEFORE, shows that the raw pointer does not count as a reference, just the shared_ptr that owns the resource.

The next two results, showing 1 and the word AFTER, occurred after the deletion of the two raw pointers pA and pB. Even with the deletion of pA and pB, the instances of the C++ class Person previously assigned to these two raw pointers were not destroyed.

This is because the shared_ptr smart pointers spPersonA and spPersonB own the resources, in this case, the two instances of the C++ class Person.

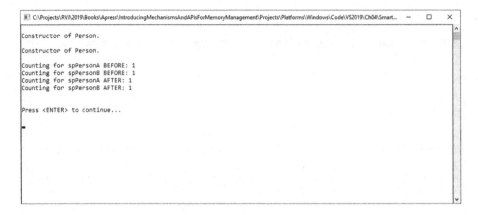

Figure 4-46. *Showing the results of reference counting of spPersonA and spPersonB, without using a weak_ptr*

Figure 4-47 shows two `weak_ptr` smart pointers taking ownership of the resources without incrementing the reference counter.

In this sequence, we have the `weak_ptr` `wpPersonA` temporarily taking ownership of `spPersonA`, and `wpPersonB` temporarily taking ownership of `spPersonB`, without incrementing the reference counter for the shared pointers.

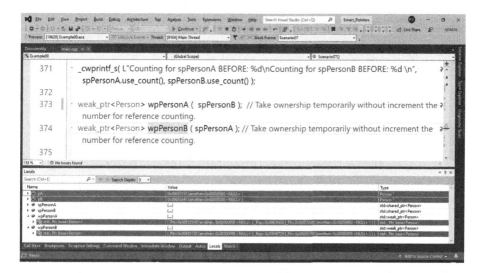

Figure 4-47. *Here we have the weak_ptr wpPersonA temporarily taking ownership of spPersonA, and wpPersonB temporarily taking ownership of spPersonB, without incrementing the reference counter for shared pointers*

Figure 4-48 shows the sequence of code where the reference counters for weak_ptr smart pointer are demonstrated.

In this sequence, if weak_ptr is still valid, that is, not expired yet, it has the same value for reference counting as the shared_ptr owned temporarily by it, in this case, the value is 1, as we can see in the first four results.

The reference counters for shared_ptr are not changed when we have a weak_ptr smart pointer owning a resource via a shared_ptr smart pointer.

```
C:\Projects\RVJ\2019\Books\Apress\IntroducingMechanismsAndAPIsForMemoryManagement\Projects\Platforms\Windows\Code\VS2019\Ch04\Smart...   —   □   ×
Now, using weak_ptr

Counting for spPersonA BEFORE: 1
Counting for spPersonB BEFORE: 1
Counting for spPersonA AFTER: 1
Counting for spPersonB AFTER: 1
Destructor of Person.

Counting for wpPersonA AFTER: 1
Counting for wpPersonB AFTER: 0
Counting for spPersonA AFTER: 1
Counting for spPersonB AFTER: 0
Counting for wpPersonA AFTER reset: 0
Counting for wpPersonB AFTER reset: 0
Counting for spPersonA AFTER reset of wpPersonA: 1
Counting for spPersonB AFTER reset of wpPersonB: 0
Destructor of Person.


Press <ENTER> to finish...
```

Figure 4-48. *Showing the results of reference counting of spPersonA and spPersonB, using a weak_ptr*

Summary

Here we list some recommendations for using smart pointers.

Do's

- Do consider using raw pointers when necessary.

- Do minimize the use of weak_ptr smart pointers.

- Do use smart pointers if you're having difficulties with raw pointers.

Don'ts

- Don't use algorithms that depend on cyclic pointers, cyclic references, and cyclic smart pointers of any type.

- Don't replace raw pointers with smart pointers where raw pointers are a requirement.

- Don't try to modify the natural purpose of each smart pointer.

- Don't try to encapsulate a `unique_ptr` just to modify the aspect of a single reference.

CHAPTER 5

Working with Lvalue and Rvalue References

In this chapter, you will learn about C++ references, specifically about C++ lvalue and rvalue references.

Purpose of a C++ Reference

In one word, the purpose of a C++ reference is *efficiency*.

Additionally, C++ references reduce syntactical complexity, and developers experience difficulties and insecurity when dealing directly with raw pointers.

A C++ reference stores a memory address.

A C++ reference, as well as a pointer, stores a memory address. The difference between a pointer and a reference is that, once initialized, a C++ reference cannot refer to another item and cannot be assigned a `nullptr` (C++) or `NULL` (C/C++) value.

The ampersand (&) symbol, or "E commercial" as it is known in Brazil, is a C++ reference when used with the syntax described in this chapter.

- When applied, the & operator means a C++ lvalue reference.

- When applied, the && operator means a C++ rvalue reference.

We will be working with two types of C++ references: lvalue and rvalue. But we also have a prvalue reference, a glvalue reference, and an xvalue reference.

- A C++ prvalue reference means a pure rvalue reference.

- A C++ glvalue reference means a generalized value reference.

- A C++ xvalue reference means an expiring value reference.

Argument Value Passing

We have three ways for argument values to be passed between functions:

- When passing an argument value by value, a copy of the argument value is made. The function receiving the copy works on this local copy and not on the original value. The original value remains preserved.

- When passing an argument value via a pointer, the memory address where the original argument value is stored is supplied as the argument value. With this information in the memory address, the changes made by the function are also visible to the original variable.

- When passing an argument value by reference, the memory address where the original argument value is stored is also supplied as the argument value. With this information in the memory address, the changes made by the function are also visible to the original variable.

Passing an Argument Value by Value

First let's talk about passing an argument value by value.

A copy of the original value is made, and the changes are local and do not update the original value.

In our examples, we will be using a simple data struct named _Data, as shown in Listing 5-1 and Figure 5-1.

Listing 5-1. Simple Data Struct Used by Examples

```
struct _Data {

        uint32_t Id;

} Information;
```

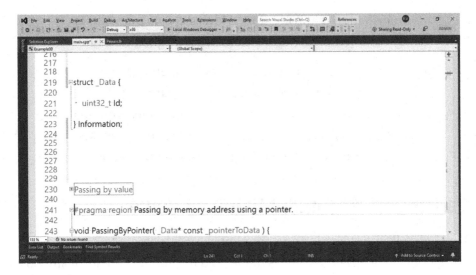

Figure 5-1. *Data structure _Data used with the example*

Open the sample solution named <install folder>\ Platforms\ Windows\Code\Ch05\References\References.sln.

In the project Example00, open the main.cpp source code file.

The Example00\main.cpp source code file contains various functions that show how to pass argument values. Each of these functions can be executed independently.

Listing 5-2 shows the PassingByValue() function and the example of passing an argument value by value.

Listing 5-2. Passing an Argument Value by Value

```
#pragma region Include Files

#include <cstdlib>
#include <cstdint>

#include <Utils.h>

#pragma endregion
```

```
#pragma region Namespaces

using namespace std;

#pragma endregion

#pragma region Sample data structure

struct _Data {

        uint32_t Id;

} Information;

#pragma endregion

#pragma region Passing by value

void PassingByValue( _Data _localData ) {

        _localData.Id = 2000ui32;

        return;
};

#pragma endregion

void wmain() {

        _Data _mainData { 5000ui32 };

        ::PassingByValue( _mainData );

        ::Pause( true );

        return;
};
```

The _localData parameter gets a copy of the original instance of the data struct and all the information associated with this instance. This means that all changes are made in the local copy with function scope, and the original data of the source instance is not changed. The sequence is shown in Figure 5-2, Figure 5-3, and Figure 5-4: a value is supplied, passed by value, changed inside the function, and returned with the original value.

Figure 5-2 shows the state before the argument value's copy is informed.

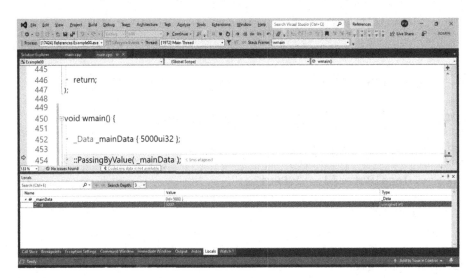

Figure 5-2. *State before the argument value's copy is informed*

Figure 5-3 shows the sequence where the _localData function parameter gets a copy of the original instance of the data struct _Data and all the information associated with this instance, which was informed as an argument value.

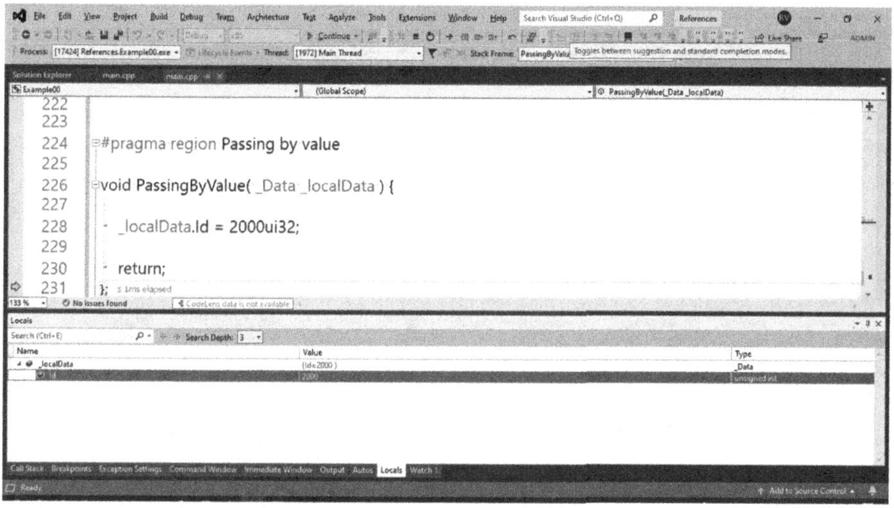

Figure 5-3. *The function updates the local data copy but not the original value*

Inside the PassingByValue() function, through the _localData argument, the value assigned to the _Data.Id field changes to 2000ui32. The original value was 5000ui32.

Figure 5-4 shows the sequence where the PassingByValue() function has returned to the wmain() function.

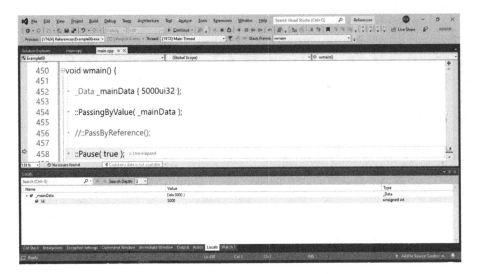

Figure 5-4. *The original value is still part of the state of the original variable*

Inside the `PassingByValue()` function, we have changed the instance value of the `_Data.Id` field to `2000ui32`, but returning to the `wmain()` function, the instance value of the `_Data.Id` field is preserved to `5000ui32`, which is the original `_Data.Id` field instance value.

This sequence shows that when we are using data passed by value, the original instance values are copied to a local copy inside the called function.

This local copy is accessed through the parameter declared on the function signature, like with `_localData` in the `PassingByValue()` sample function.

Because of this, inside the called function we are working with a local copy and not accessing the original instance with the original data. Therefore, the original data is preserved between the calls of the function, and the local changes are visible only to the local copy.

Passing an Argument Value by Pointer

Let's now discuss how to pass an argument value via a pointer.

Within this scenario we are passing the memory address where the instance data value is stored. The changes are also seen by any pointer variable pointing to the same memory address where the argument value is stored.

Listing 5-3 shows the PassingByPointer() function, and Figure 5-5, Figure 5-6, Figure 5-7, and Figure 5-8 show the sequence of execution.

Listing 5-3. Implementation of PassingByPointer() Function

```
#pragma region Include Files

#include <cstdlib>
#include <cstdint>

#include <Utils.h>

#pragma endregion

#pragma region Passing by memory address using a pointer.

void PassingByPointer( _Data* const _pointerToData ) {

        if ( _pointerToData != nullptr ) _pointerToData->Id =
        200ui32;

        /*

        Or using other option for pointer syntax.

        if ( _pointerToData !=nullptr ) ( *_pointerToData ).Id =
        200ui32;

        */

        return;
};
```

```
#pragma endregion

void wmain() {

        _Data _mainData { 5000ui32 };

        /*

        Pass the memory address where the instance values of
        data structure are currently stored.

        */
        ::PassingByPointer( &_mainData );

        return;
};
```

Figure 5-5 shows the sequence where an instance of the struct _Data is created and initialized with sample data, and this instance of struct _Data is accessed through the local variable named _mainData.

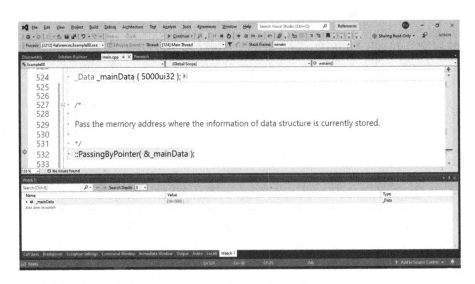

Figure 5-5. *Supplying the argument value via a pointer*

The source code sequence is using the `PassingByPointer()` function that receives the memory address where the instance of the struct `_Data` is stored as an argument value.

Figure 5-6 shows the sequence where `PassingByPointer()` has declared a pointer to the struct `_Data` as a parameter.

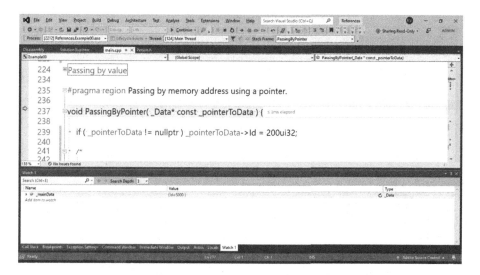

Figure 5-6. *The state of the argument value right before the change*

This means that the argument value received by the `_pointerToData` pointer type argument is a memory address; more precisely, it's the memory address where an instance of the struct `_Data` is stored.

The modifier `const` is used to guarantee that once assigned to the pointer local variable, this memory address value will not be changed by another memory address. This is a rule used for security reasons.

Using the `const` modifier avoids the unwanted modification of a memory address once assigned to a pointer variable, because this kind of change can be used to inform a memory address of viruses or any kind of bad software routine installed on the machine where the executable code is running.

Figure 5-7 shows a sequence where a new value is assigned to the
_Data->Id instance field.

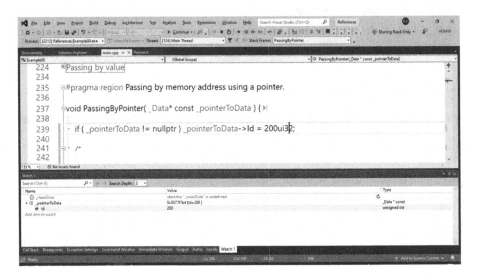

Figure 5-7. *The state of the argument value right after the change*

Notice that the syntax to access the data field is different because we
are using a pointer type variable, not a nonpointer type variable.

Another aspect is that now we are working directly on the original data
stored in memory because we are working with a pointer to this memory
localization where the data instance is stored, not in a local copy created
only for use inside the function.

Any change made here is visible to any other variable that has access to
this same instance.

Figure 5-8 shows the sequence where the PassingByPointer()
function returns from the call, and the _mainData local variable is
accessing instance data modified by the sequence executed inside the
PassingByPointer() function.

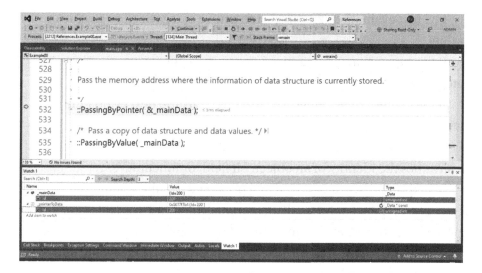

Figure 5-8. *The state of the argument value right after returning and with the changes*

In fact, `_mainData` inside the `wmain()` function and `_pointerToData` inside the `PassingByPointer()` function are accessing the same instance data in the same memory location.

Passing an Argument Value by Reference

Let's now discuss how to pass an argument value by reference.

But before we learn how to pass by reference, we need to understand some terminology.

As shown in Figure 5-9, in the C++ programming language structure, there is a taxonomy for expressions: lvalue and rvalue are two of these categories (and are not value-related terms). Historically, lvalue and rvalue expressions are so named like this because they can appear on the left side or right side of an assignment. However, this is no longer a general rule. In the current taxonomy, the other categories for the classification of expressions are glvalue (generalized lvalue), prvalue (pure rvalue), and xvalue (expiring lvalue).

In a first evaluation, an expression can be categorized as glvalue or rvalue.

If the expression is categorized as a glvalue, the next evaluation can categorize it as an lvalue or xvalue.

If the expression is categorized as an rvalue, the next evaluation can categorize it as a prvalue or xvalue.

An expression is categorized as a glvalue when the evaluation determines the identity of an object, bit field, or function.

An expression is categorized as a prvalue when the evaluation initializes an object or bit field or computes the value of an operator's operand according to the context in which it appears.

An expression is categorized as an xvalue when it is a glvalue that denotes an object or bit field that can be reused, usually because its life span is about to end.

Certain types of expressions that have rvalue references are transformed into xvalue references, such as the call of a function whose return type is a rvalue reference.

To end, an lvalue expression is a glvalue expression that is not an xvalue expression, and an rvalue expression is a prvalue expression or is an xvalue expression.

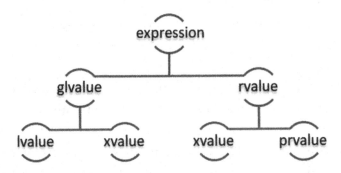

Figure 5-9. *Taxonomy for expression classification in the C++ programming language*

Like with passing by pointer, when passing an argument value by reference, we are also passing the memory address where the value is stored, but the syntax is simpler. Different from a pointer, once assigned, the reference cannot point to another item, and nullptr (C++) or NULL (C/C++) cannot be assigned to a reference.

Working with an Lvalue Reference

An lvalue reference is accessible in the scope of the declaration and initialization of the reference.

Shown in Listing 5-4, there is a variable of type _Data that is our data struct to be supplied by reference.

A function named PassingByReference() has a reference to _Data as the argument value.

Declared and initialized with the memory address where the instance of _Data is stored, we have the local variable named _localData, which receives the argument value by reference. This sequence is also shown in Figure 5-10, Figure 5-11, and Figure 5-12.

Listing 5-4. Implementation of PassingByReference() Sample Function

```
#pragma region Include Files

#include <cstdlib>
#include <cstdio>
#include <cwchar>
#include <cstdint>
#include <cstring>

#include <Utils.h>

#pragma endregion
```

```
#pragma region Passing by reference

void PassingByReference( _Data& _localData ) {

        _localData.Id = 300ui32;

        return;
}

#pragma endregion

void wmain() {

_Data _mainData { 5000ui32 };

::PassingByReference( _mainData );

        return;
};
```

Figure 5-10 shows the sequence where an instance of the struct _Data is accessed via reference.

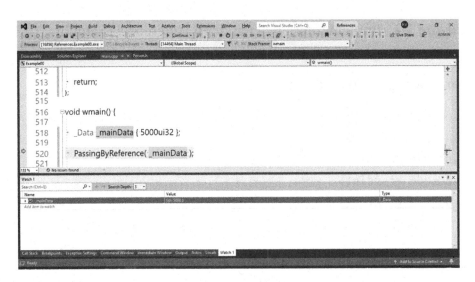

Figure 5-10. *Supplying the memory address where the data struct instance values are stored*

A reference provides the same efficiency of a pointer, but without the complexity of the syntax of pointers.

In the sequence, the syntax is assuming that we are passing a memory address, because the signature of the PassingByReference() function is using a parameter of type reference.

Figure 5-11 shows the sequence where the argument value received by the function parameter _localData is a reference, that is, a memory address.

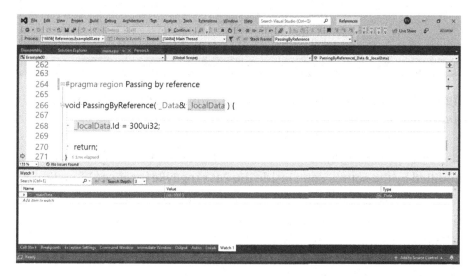

Figure 5-11. *Updating the original data values via reference*

As we can see in the source code, we are using the same syntax as with a nonpointer variable, but we are modifying the original instance data, because we are working directly on the memory location where the instance data is stored.

As shown in Figure 5-12, we can read a sequence where the PassingByReference() function has returned to the wmain() function.

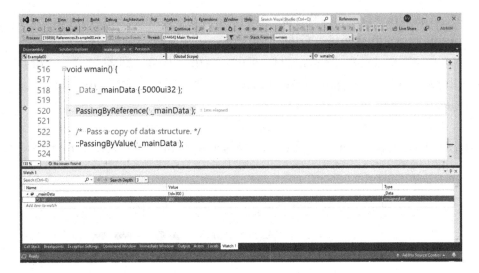

Figure 5-12. *On the return, the state of the instance appears as updated*

Notice that the original value for the `_Data.Id` instance field was modified by the source code inside the `PassingByReference()` function.

Every change is reflected for all "sides," which means that every variable with a reference to or a pointer to the original variable, will see the updates made through the function.

Working with an Rvalue Reference

An rvalue reference creates a temporary object as a result of the complete or partial evaluation of an expression. This temporary object occurs during certain intermediate steps required for the expression to generate a complete result.

As shown in Listing 5-5 and in Listing 5-6, the xvalue (eXpiring) reference is used and afterward becomes a rvalue.

As a result, a temporary object is first created to satisfy the need for the lvalue expression. Next, this temporary object of type `_Data` is initialized. After creating and initializing this temporary object of type `_Data`, in the context, we have an lvalue reference declared and initialized with this temporary object. In the example code, the variable with the name _localData is declared and defined as an rvalue reference to an instance of _Data.

As shown in Listing 5-7, the result is the automatic calling of the move constructor with the argument value rvalue supplied and used to initialize a new instance of _Data.

Listing 5-5. Implementation of _Data.h Header File

```
#pragma once

#pragma region Include Files

#include <cstdint>

#pragma endregion

struct _Data {

public:
    uint32_t Id {};

public:

    _Data() { return; };
    _Data( uint32_t __newId ) : _Data() {
        Id = __newId;
        return;
    };

    _Data( const _Data& __other ) noexcept : _Data
    ( __other.Id ) {

        _cwprintf_s( L"Copying..." );

        return;
    };
```

```
    _Data( _Data&& __other ) noexcept : _Data( __other.Id ) {

        _cwprintf_s( L"Moving..." );

        return;
    };
};
```

Listing 5-6. Implementation of ByReference.cpp Source Code File

```
#pragma region Include Files

#include <cstdlib>
#include <cstdint>

#include <conio.h>

#include <Utils.h>

#include "_Data.h"

#pragma endregion

#pragma region Passing by reference

void PassingByReference( _Data& _localData ) {

        _localData.Id = 300ui32;

        return;
};

#pragma endregion

#pragma region Get a rvalue.

_Data GetARvalue() {

        _Data _localData { 100ui32 };
```

```
    /* Using a xvalue for this example. */
    return _localData;
};
```

#pragma endregion

Listing 5-7. Implementation of main.cpp

```
#pragma region Include Files

#include <cstdlib>
#include <cstdint>

#include <Utils.h>

#include "_Data.h"
#include "ByReference.h"

#pragma endregion

#pragma region Namespaces

using namespace std;

#pragma endregion

extern "C++" void PassingByReference( _Data& _localData );
extern "C++" _Data GetARvalue();

void wmain() {

    _Data myData( ::GetRvalue( ) );

    ::Pause( true );

    return;

};
```

CHAPTER 6

Working with Microsoft CRT/ UCRT and Memory Management

In this chapter, you will learn about the CRT/UCRT and functionalities for memory management.

Microsoft CRT/UCRT and Memory Management

The Microsoft CRT/UCRT implementation is a set of functions, data structures, and runtimes that encapsulate functionalities and provide facilities for a variety of activities. These activities include memory management tasks such as memory allocation, reallocation, getting information about the blocks of memory, and the release of blocks of memory.

© Roger Villela 2020
R. Villela, *Introducing Mechanisms and APIs for Memory Management*,
https://doi.org/10.1007/978-1-4842-5416-5_6

- The Microsoft UCRT includes only the functions and data structures that can be used by UWP applications and with WinRT components.

- The Microsoft CRT includes functions and data structures that, by definition, can be used with any kind of applications and/or components.

- The Microsoft CRT/UCRT can manage memory for memory segment heaps and stacks.

Heap Management

Collectively, every set of memory addresses located in dynamic RAM and that can be used to dynamically store and manage generic data is called a *heap*.

These memory blocks on heaps are managed throughout the Microsoft CRT/UCRT runtime and algorithms and are collectively named CRT/UCRT heap memory blocks and are called a CRT/UCRT heap.

In general, a heap is represented by a data structure of a tree in computer engineering algorithms, with a conceptual virtual root node and sets of conceptual virtual left and right nodes. All of these root nodes, left nodes, and right nodes are linked together through some criteria based on the management technique used to work with the memory blocks.

We not only can allocate a memory block but also can reallocate a block of memory, for a bigger size or for a smaller size, depending on the situation.

A block of memory can also have zero as a size. In fact, we can allocate a block of memory with an initial zero size without checking an initial condition and after some checks expand the size of block of memory using some contextual criteria. This scenario is interesting when working with complex multithreaded code and rules that are applied at different times and based on the same source code.

Working with Allocation

Internally, the Microsoft CRT/UCRT Heap Management functions use the Microsoft Windows API Heap Management functions and data structures.

The Microsoft CRT/UCRT Heap Management API simplifies the use of the Microsoft Windows API for heap management through a more objective and compact public API. The Microsoft CRT/UCRT Heap Management API hides repetitive tasks related to heap management and with the Windows API for heap management can create and delete heaps.

Listing 6-1 shows an example of the malloc() memory allocation function. The malloc() function returns a void pointer to the allocated memory block.

If an error occurs through the allocation process, such as because of insufficient memory, then the nullptr (C++) value is returned instead of a void pointer. The error code can be retrieved via the errno() macro to get more detailed information about the error condition.

For the return of function be different from void *, use the type cast in the return value such as BaseType* buffer = reinterpret_cast< BaseType* > (malloc(BUFFER_SIZE)), for example.

The total number of allocated bytes is slightly larger than the value reported as an argument. This is because a little more space is required for alignment conditions and maintenance information on the allocations made through the Microsoft CRT/UCRT and the memory management engine of the operating system.

It is important to remember that the malloc() function is a public interface for the actual implementation that is in a file named malloc_base.cpp and in a public interface file named malloc.cpp, with the calls for the debug and release implementations.

The files `malloc_base.cpp` and `malloc.cpp` are part of the source code of Microsoft CRT/UCRT at `<Drive Letter>:\Windows Kits\10\Source\10.0.18362.0\ucrt\heap\`. This implementation is distributed with the Microsoft Windows SDK and Microsoft Visual Studio versions, including recent versions such as Microsoft Visual Studio 2017 and Microsoft Visual Studio 2019.

In the file `malloc_base.cpp`, some simple checks on the value reported in the size argument are made, and the Microsoft Windows API heap `HeapAlloc()` function performs the actual allocation work.

The Microsoft CRT/UCRT `malloc()` function, both the debug and release implementations, use the Windows API `HeapAlloc()` function that is part of the functionality of the Microsoft operating system component called Heap Manager.

The `HeapAlloc()` function is part of the Windows API functionality group for memory management called Heap Management functions.

The functions and data structures in this group are part of the Windows operating system component called Heap Manager.

The Heap Manager component is one of the high-level components of Microsoft Windows operating system; it facilitates interaction with the most advanced APIs for memory management.

On return, the Microsoft CRT/UCRT evaluates and tries to simplify the information by indicating `nullptr` (C++), an error code, and one more message. With this, the code is less prone to error, mainly dealing with the code complexities in advanced programming languages and projections such as C, C++, C++/CX, C++/CLI, Assembly, and CIL Common Intermediate Language (CLR).

Listing 6-1. Example of malloc() Memory Allocation Function

```
#ifdef __INTEL_COMPILER
#pragma warning( disable: 1079; )
#else
#pragma warning (disable : 6011 6387 6308 6386 28183 )
#endif
#pragma region Include Files

#include <cstdio>
#include <cstdlib>
#include <cstdint>
#include <cerrno>

#include <malloc.h>
#include <conio.h>
#include <strsafe.h>
#include <Utils.h>

/*MFC*/

#include <afx.h>

#pragma endregion
#pragma region Support functions
/*

Shows information about allocation.

*/
void PrintAllocationStatus( void* const target ) {

        if ( target != nullptr ) {

                ::uint32_t allocatedBytes { ( ( ::uint32_t ) _
                msize( reinterpret_cast< void* >( target ) ) ) };
                /*
```

```
                    The malloc(), calloc(), and realloc() functions
                    assigns the ENOMEM value for errno() macro if the
                    allocation fails or if the value for requested
                    memory exceeds the value of _HEAP_MAXREQ.

                    */

                    ::_cwprintf_s( reinterpret_cast< const wchar_t*
                    const >( u"Memory Requested > _HEAP_MAXREQ ?
                    %s\n\nSize: %u byte(s)\n" ),
                            ( ( allocatedBytes > _HEAP_MAXREQ ) ?
                            u"true" : u"false" ), allocatedBytes );

            };

            return;
    };
    #pragma endregion

    #pragma region Base Type definition
    typedef char16_t BaseType;
    #pragma endregion

    /* Maximum number of items in the allocated block. */
    #if defined( _WIN32 )
    constexpr ::uint32_t Length { 80ui32 };
    constexpr ::uint32_t BaseTypeSizeInBytes { sizeof( BaseType ) };
    #elif _WIN64
    constexpr ::uint64_t Length { 80ui64 };
    constexpr ::uint64_t BaseTypeSizeInBytes { sizeof( BaseType ) };
    #endif
```

```
/* Maximum size of allocated block of memory, in bytes. */
constexpr ::uint32_t BufferSize { BaseTypeSizeInBytes * Length
};

void wmain() {

BaseType* buffer {};
::int32_t lastError { -1i32 };

#pragma region malloc()/free() functions

        buffer = reinterpret_cast< BaseType* > ( ::malloc( ( (
        ::size_t ) BufferSize ) ) ), lastError = errno;

if ( ( buffer == nullptr ) && ( lastError == ENOMEM ) )
::_cwprintf_s ( reinterpret_cast< const wchar_t* const >(
u"Allocation fail. ENOMEM error code...\n" ) );
else {

        if ( buffer != nullptr ) ::SecureZeroMemory(
        reinterpret_cast< PVOID >( buffer ), ( ( SIZE_T )
        BufferSize ) );

        if ( buffer != nullptr ) ::StringCchCopy( ( reinterpret_
        cast< ::STRSAFE_LPWSTR >( buffer ) ), ( ( size_t )
        Length ), reinterpret_cast< ::STRSAFE_LPCWSTR >(
        u"malloc and free" ) );

        if ( buffer != nullptr ) ::_cwprintf_s( reinterpret_
        cast< const wchar_t* const >( u"Buffer: %s\n\nSize (in
        char16_t): %u characters\n\n" ), reinterpret_cast< const
        wchar_t* const >( buffer ), ( ( ( ::uint32_t )::_msize(
        buffer ) ) / BaseTypeSizeInBytes ) );
```

```
        if ( buffer != nullptr ) ::SecureZeroMemory(
        reinterpret_cast< PVOID >( buffer ), ( ( SIZE_T )
        BufferSize ) );

        ::PrintAllocationStatus( reinterpret_cast< void* >
        ( buffer ) );

        ::Pause();
};

#pragma endregion

        ::Pause( true );

        return;
};
```

Listing 6-2 shows all the implementation code in the `malloc.cpp` source code file, except the header files.

Listing 6-2. Implementation Code in malloc.cpp (Except Header Files)

```
// Allocates a block of memory of size 'size' bytes in the
heap.  If allocation
// fails, nullptr is returned.
extern "C" _CRTRESTRICT void* __cdecl malloc(size_t const size)
{
        #ifdef _DEBUG
        return _malloc_dbg(size, _NORMAL_BLOCK, nullptr, 0);
```

```
#else
return _malloc_base(size);
#endif
}
```

Listing 6-3 shows all the implementation code in the malloc_base.cpp
source code file, except the header files.

Listing 6-3. All Implementation Code of malloc_base.cpp (Except
Header Files)

```
// This function implements the logic of malloc().  It is
called directly by the
        // malloc() function in the Release CRT and is called by
        the debug heap in the
        // Debug CRT.
        extern "C" _CRTRESTRICT void* __cdecl _malloc_
        base(size_t const size)
        {
                // Ensure that the requested size is not too
                large:
                _VALIDATE_RETURN_NOEXC(_HEAP_MAXREQ >= size,
                ENOMEM, nullptr);

                // Ensure we request an allocation of at least
                one byte:
                size_t const actual_size = size == 0 ? 1 : size;

                for (;;)
                {
                        void* const block = HeapAlloc(__acrt_heap,
                        0, actual_size);
```

```
if (block)
        return block;

// Otherwise, see if we need to call the
new handler, and if so call it.
// If the new handler fails, just return
nullptr:
if (_query_new_mode() == 0 || !_callnewh
(actual_size))
{
        errno = ENOMEM;
        return nullptr;
}

// The new handler was successful; try to
allocate again...
    }
}
```

Note that the code is a kind of dialogue between the Microsoft CRT/
UCRT infrastructure and the Windows API for memory management; in
this case, it is one of the various heap functions.

Functions that handle the heap blocks in turn converge with a more
advanced level of API for memory management implemented in Microsoft
Windows; they are named *virtual functions*.

The sequence, very simplistically, looks like this:

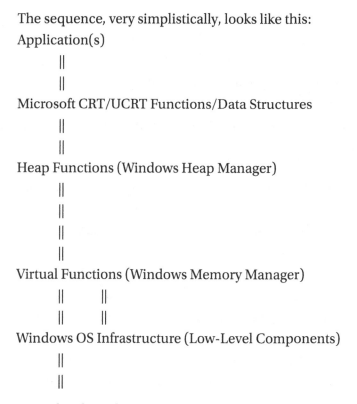

Application(s)

‖
‖

Microsoft CRT/UCRT Functions/Data Structures

‖
‖

Heap Functions (Windows Heap Manager)

‖
‖
‖
‖

Virtual Functions (Windows Memory Manager)

‖   ‖
‖   ‖

Windows OS Infrastructure (Low-Level Components)

‖
‖

Specialized Hardware and Components for Memory Management on Device (PC, Windows Phone, Tablet, Xbox, and So On)

Applications and libraries can safely use the memory management functions that are available through the Microsoft C Runtime and/ or Universal C Runtime Library (such as malloc(), free(), calloc(), realloc(), and so on), through the C++ programming language operators such as the new and delete operators, and through other functions implemented through the C++ Standard Library. Internally, as I have previously cited, all these APIs use the functions of the Windows API for memory management, such as heap functions, virtual functions, and the specialized components of the Microsoft Windows operating system, such as the Heap Manager and Windows Memory Manager.

Similarly, the CLR, COM, and WinRT platforms use these features of the Microsoft Windows operating system to implement their sophisticated mechanisms for memory management. Even platforms and products of third parties such as Java and Embarcadero Delphi use the Microsoft CRT/UCRT API or directly call the Windows API memory management functions when required by its architectures and engineering implementation techniques.

The main difference (and advantage) between using these functions of the Microsoft CRT/UCRT and directly using the memory management functions of the Windows API, such as heap functions and virtual functions, is that they are accessed by specialized functionality and control.

For example, through virtual functions, we can "clear" a block of memory from the previous content preparing for a new allocation and can perform an undo, given certain conditions, and all the deleted content can be retrieved and reassigned to the original block of memory.

A disadvantage, however, is that the advanced features directly utilize the memory management functions of the Windows API, such as heap functions and virtual functions, requiring more knowledge about the architecture of the operating system and hardware.

Working with Reallocation

One example of an advanced feature is the reallocation behavior. We can reallocate a block of memory various times using the Microsoft CRT/UCRT `realloc()` function.

To this, we need to first allocate a block of memory on the Microsoft CRT/UCRT heap using the `malloc()`, `calloc()`, or `realloc()` function.

After this first allocation, if necessary, we can reallocate with a smaller size or a larger size than the original, as shown in the source code in Listing 6-4 that's double the size of a buffer during the reallocation step.

Listing 6-4. Example of Sequence to Use for realloc() Microsoft CRT/UCRT Function

```
#ifdef __INTEL_COMPILER
#pragma warning( disable: 1079; )
#else
#pragma warning(disable: 6066 6308 6273 6011 6387 6385 28182
28183 )
#endif

#pragma region Include Files

#include <conio.h>
#include <Utils.h>

#include <cstdlib>
#include <cstdio>
#include <cstdint>
#include <cstring>
#include <memory>

#pragma endregion

#pragma region Namespaces
using namespace std;
#pragma endregion

typedef char16_t BaseType;

constexpr uint32_t BaseTypeSize { sizeof( BaseType ) };

/* Base Number of items in buffer. */
constexpr uint32_t NumberOfElements { 100ui32 };

/* Initial Size of block of memory , in bytes. */
constexpr uint32_t Length { ( NumberOfElements * BaseTypeSize ) };
```

179

```cpp
#pragma region Support functions
/*

Functions that shows the values stored in a block of memory.

*/
void PrintContent( BaseType* const memBlock ) {

        uint32_t count { ( ( uint32_t ) _msize( reinterpret_
        cast< void* >( memBlock ) ) / BaseTypeSize ) };

        for ( uint32_t index {}; index != count; index++ )
                _cwprintf_s( reinterpret_cast< const wchar_t*
                const >( u"buffer[ %u ]: %C\n" ), index, *( (
                memBlock ) +index ) );

        return;
};

#pragma endregion

void wmain() {

        /*

        Before do the reallocation, make a copy of the address
        of the pointer that will be reallocated.
        The address can be other after the reallocation.

        */

        BaseType* buffer { ( reinterpret_cast<BaseType* >(
        malloc( ( ( size_t ) Length ) ) ) ) };
        BaseType* backup { reinterpret_cast<BaseType* >(
        SecureZeroMemory( reinterpret_cast< PVOID >( buffer ), (
        ( SIZE_T ) Length ) ) ) };
```

```
buffer = ( reinterpret_cast<BaseType* >( wmemset( reinterpret_
cast< wchar_t* >( buffer ), L'*', ( ( size_t ) NumberOfElements
) ) ) );

PrintContent( reinterpret_cast<BaseType* const >( buffer ) );

        _cwprintf_s( reinterpret_cast< const wchar_t* const
        >( u"\nSize of buffer: %u byte(s)\n\n" ), _msize(
        reinterpret_cast<void*>( buffer ) ) );

::Pause( {} );
        /*

        The realloc() function can use another memory LOCATION
        to allocate the memory block.

        */

        _cwprintf_s( reinterpret_cast< const wchar_t* const > (
        u"(before)Start address of buffer: %#0x\n(before)Start
        address of backup: %#0x\n" ),
                &buffer, &backup );

        ::Pause( {} );

                /*

                Try the relocation, double the size, and check if
                it worked...

                */
        if ( ( buffer = reinterpret_cast< BaseType* >(
        realloc( reinterpret_cast< void* >( buffer ), _msize(
        reinterpret_cast< void* >( buffer ) ) << 1ui32 ) ) ) ==
        nullptr ) {
```

```cpp
        _cwprintf_s( reinterpret_cast< const wchar_t*
        const >( u"_HEAP_MAXREQ: %#0x byte(s)\nerrno
        value: %d\n" ), _HEAP_MAXREQ, errno );

        free( reinterpret_cast< void* >( backup ) ),
        backup = nullptr;

} else {
        uint32_t newSize = _msize( ( void* ) buffer );

        _cwprintf_s( reinterpret_cast< const wchar_t*
        const >( u"buffer value: %s\nbuffer total new
        size in bytes: %u\n\n" ), buffer, newSize );

        buffer = reinterpret_cast< BaseType* > (
        SecureZeroMemory( reinterpret_cast< PVOID >( buffer
        + NumberOfElements ), ( SIZE_T ) Length ) );
        buffer -= NumberOfElements;

        _cwprintf_s( reinterpret_cast< const wchar_t*
        const >( u"buffer value: %s\nbuffer total new size
        in bytes: %u\n\n" ), buffer, _msize( buffer ) );

        buffer = reinterpret_cast< BaseType* >(
        wmemset( reinterpret_cast< wchar_t* >( &buffer[
        NumberOfElements ] ), L'#', ( ( size_t )
        NumberOfElements ) ) );

    free( reinterpret_cast< void* >( buffer -
    NumberOfElements ) );

};
```

```
    buffer = nullptr, backup = nullptr;

    ::Pause( true );

    return;
};
```

Do's

The following are the do's:

- Do use the Microsoft CRT/UCRT functions and data structures with the C programming language.

- Do use the Microsoft CRT/UCRT functions and data structures with the C++ programming language.

- Do use the Microsoft UCRT functions and data structures with C++/CX projection.

- Do use the Microsoft CRT functions and data structures with C++/CLI projection.

- Do use the Microsoft UCRT functions and data structures on UWP applications and/or WinRT components.

- Do use the `reinterpret_cast<>` operator for casting the return of the `malloc()`, `calloc()`, and `realloc()` functions.

Don'ts

The following are the don'ts:

- Don't work with allocations without checks for `nullptr` return value and error conditions.

- Don't work with reallocation without checking the return value for `nullptr`.

- Don't work with reallocation without checking the error code for the operation, such as `ENOMEM` for insufficient memory.

Index

© Roger Villela 2020
R. Villela, *Introducing Mechanisms and APIs for Memory Management*,
https://doi.org/10.1007/978-1-4842-5416-5

P

Q

R, S, T

U

V, W, X, Y, Z

Printed in the United States
By Bookmasters